Karate Stupid
A True Story of Survival

Scott Langley

Contents

This book details the author's personal experiences and opinions about those experiences. Some names and identifying details have been changed to protect the privacy of individuals.

The author and publisher are providing this book and its contents on an "as is" basis and make no representations or warranties of any kind with respect to this book or its contents. The author and publisher disclaim all such representations and warranties, including for example warranties of advice for a particular purpose. Except as specifically stated in this book, neither the author or publisher, nor any authors, contributors, or other representatives will be liable for damages arising out of or in connection with the use of this book. This is a comprehensive limitation of liability that applies to all damages of any kind, including (without limitation) compensatory; direct, indirect or consequential damages; loss of data, income or profit; loss of or damage to property and claims of third parties.

You understand that this book is not intended as a substitute for your own experiences of similar or identical experiences to those of the author.

Typesetting by FormattingExperts.com

For Tor and Doireann

In Autumn 2013 I sent this book to my Sensei in Japan for their approval. They responded immediately declaring the book to be full of lies and misrepresentations of Japan and forbid me to publish it. I was suspended for a month and then effectively expelled in January 2014. Suddenly, my 30 year relationship with Japanese karate had abruptly come to an end. This had been a part of my entire karate life and I had dedicated myself to its values and rules, running the karate organisation in Ireland for over ten years. I would never have wanted to jeopardise my position or damage the reputation of the group. However, unfortunately, the sacrifices I made during this true story are nothing compared to the sacrifices I've had to make to publish it.

Scott Langley
30th January 2013

In Japan people are often described as *karate-baka* – karate-stupid. That is, they are stupid enough to do karate. This is the story of how stupid I am.

Chapter One:

Tremors and Tears

It is summer 1997 and I'm boarding the plane to Tokyo. I'm weighing up the pros and cons of teaching English in Japan, although I know that it's far too late to be making such vital decisions. I have been promised a job, an apartment and a year-long visa. As well as this, for the first time in my life, I will have a salary. What could be better? On the other hand, I know no one there. I can't speak the language. My girlfriend, Jen, who is coming too, is relying on me and the very lines that I used to chat her up are now coming back to haunt me.

'Tokyo? Yeah, what I haven't seen or done there isn't worth seeing nor doing.' I'm going straight to hell for that one.

I was twenty-four and had finished at Keele University the previous summer. Having graduated with a 2:1 in geography and anthropology, I had managed to build up huge debt in the guise of student loans – a direct correlation to the amount of alcohol I drank. I had also practiced karate almost seven days a week, three of those with Ishii Sensei, the insanely talented UK Chief Karate Instructor, at his private dojo – *basically the local village hall* – ten miles from campus. I had been captain of the university karate club, captain of the British team and European champion. I was a big fish in a small pond, as my mother constantly told me, and even my friends' endless put-downs hadn't stopped my head from expanding to planetary proportions. I was about to find out that Japan was the perfect antidote.

This wasn't my first trip to Japan. When I was nineteen and on my gap year I spent a month travelling throughout the country with Ishii Sensei. The idiosyncratic mood swings of this genius made it a fantastic but frightening experience. I had been like a child, desperate to keep up with him as he dashed from dojo to dojo encouraging fellow karate-ka to hit me. But on this, my second trip, I found out that the only thing worse than going to Japan with a madman was going without him.

We were picked up at the airport by an obscenely tall Dutchman with massive legs and a stride like the Jolly Green Giant. He took us by train to Shinjuku station, the busiest in the world – used by two million people every day – and then whisked us away to his illegally parked van. The crowds of Japanese people parted like the Red Sea as he made his way across the busiest zebra crossing on the planet while we frantically scurried behind him. He threw our suitcases into the back and then threw us in after them, so that our first glimpses of Tokyo were through a small grate in the back of an old van, sitting on our suitcases, holding on for dear life as we rattled our way to an unknown destination.

'Excuse me,' I shouted politely through the grate. 'Excuse me, where are we going?'

'Where are we going?'

'Yeah!' I confirmed in desperation.

'Here!'

With that, he pulled up at what I presumed was an estate agency because it had pictures of apartment blocks in the window. We were ushered inside and given instructions by a short, angry-looking Japanese woman. 'Sign here.'

'What is it?' The contract was all in Japanese.

'It is your contract. And I need your room deposit.' I handed over a vast amount of money and wondered, not for the first time, if this was entirely legal.

Having been thrown back into the van and after another hour of dodging bikes and pedestrians through the side streets of Tokyo, we arrived at what can only be described as a shack. Out of the van, door open, contents pulled out – including us – and again our lanky friend lurched forward, like the BFG on speed. We struggled behind him, suitcases in tow. Through the front door, we entered a dimly lit corridor. Various rooms seemed to lead off it, and the whole place brought to mind a dungeon entirely furnished by Ikea rejects. The doors consisted of sliding, rice-paper-covered bamboo frames and the floorboards creaked as if to forewarn of a ninja attack. Despite looking flimsy it gave off an air of indefinite confinement.

BFG halted at one room, opened the sliding door, allowed us to enter, and crouched down so that his head could poke under the door frame.

'Enjoy your time in Japan.' And with that turned and walked away.

Jen, whose body language had slowly changed from curiosity to worry to outright panic, gave me a horrified look. He was our only contact in Japan.

'Don't let him go.' She gripped my arm to reinforce the panic in her voice.

In an effort to appear in control, I shouted after him, 'What about a key?'

'Don't worry,' he said. 'This is Japan... perfectly safe... no need.'

Those were his last words as he sprang out of the front door, never to be seen again. Jen burst into tears.

After a desperately long time I managed to calm Jen down, and we surveyed our new abode. It took about three nanoseconds, because our single room was just short of five metres by four. It was barren except for a bookcase, a mysterious closet and a single lightbulb dangling from a frayed wire. We stood, inspecting a curious crack running the length of the floor, when suddenly our lightbulb started to sway. This was quickly followed by the whole room, to such an extent that the bookcase, had it contained any books, might have posed a serious threat of toppling over and squashing us. I stood there, unsure what to do, although getting the next train to the airport and boarding any outbound plane seemed a good option. Jen saw the look on my face.

'What's up?' she said reassuringly. 'It was probably only a lorry or something.'

'This shack is miles from any main road.' I tried to keep the hysteria from my voice.

'What are you saying?' Her face started to change.

'Jen... that was a bloody earthquake.'

'What?' She didn't wait for me to repeat myself, and after a moment's deliberation the weeping reverted to full-blown tears.

As the tremors and tears subsided, I tried to regain a bit of composure. I noticed that we had what appeared to be patio windows at one end of our room, leading onto a garden. Trying to divert attention from the natural disaster waiting to happen, I opened the windows to what I hoped would be a pretty garden, and was faced with a tiny concrete yard sporting a square-metre patch of dirt as its *pièce de resistance*. I now understood the Japanese need for bonsai trees. A woman sat in a corner in her personal fog, surrounded by butt ends, the one cigarette still on the go limply sticking from her dried-up mouth.

'Welcome to Japan,' she croaked. 'That's a lucky omen. Your first earthquake as soon as you arrive. I had to wait months.'

'Yeah, lucky.' I couldn't help but wonder if it was the same type of luck that you get when pigeons shit on you.

'You'll be Navo teachers, then,' she continued. 'I recognize that naive, fresh look anywhere. I was the same three months ago.'

'What?' This woman was anything but fresh or naive. She stood up as if it were a huge effort and ambled over to introduce herself. Her name was Sheila and she was Australian. An Aussie who was obviously missing the skin-cancer risks of back home so much that she was trying to compensate by killing herself through lung cancer was not a good start.

As the first few days slipped by, we began to meet everyone in our house. We learnt that this particular type of dwelling was officially called a '*gaijin* house', a house for foreigners. That is to say it was so old and dilapidated that no self-respecting Japanese family would be seen dead living in it. The result was that these types of places were earmarked for the *gaijin* community. By general standards, our little home was quite spacious. There were only seven of us; some places crammed in thirty or forty people. The inmates included an American, two Australians, an Irish guy and an Iranian.

Almost all were Navo or ex-Navo teachers and everyone had a look of weariness about them. The days were unbelievably hot and the house didn't have air-conditioning. Usually our new housemates would come home from a long day at school, exhausted after teaching up to six and a half hours. I wondered how they coped. During the evenings they would flake out in the communal kitchen and slag off their entire world – everyone from their bosses to their students to perverts on the trains to racist policeman asking to see their *gaijin* card for the umpteenth time. The *gaijin* (foreigner) card was a credit-card-sized identification non-Japanese were obliged to carry at all times. Unfortunately it was hardly your flexible friend. It contained your photograph, fingerprints, address and place of work and it had to be shown at every opportunity: to open a bank account, join a video shop, cross the road... The police loved to ask for it at every opportunity. I think they liked making fun of my photo.

And so I found myself living in *Tenko*. *Tenko* was TV drama from years ago, one of those dreary and oppressive programmes that the BBC churned out during the 1980s. It was about a group of women captured by the Japanese in World War II and kept in labour camps. I remember it being really hot and sticky. They were forced to eat only rice, live in a communal hut and after a hard day's work they retired to their non-air-conditioned hole to berate the world. Well that was us, and I expected any moment now one of our group would develop malaria and we'd have to perform sexual favours for our landlord to get the required medicine.

After a day or two, we plucked up the courage to venture out and explore our environs. Jafar, the Iranian, who was one of the kindest and most intelligent people I could ever have hoped to meet – he was also the only non-Navo teacher in the house – had taken us out on our first night for ice-cream and to show us around.

'So where exactly are we?' I tried to ask him this without sounding like an imbecile.

'Oh, this is Higashi-Matsubara.'

'Right. Where's that close to, then?'

He proceeded to tell us about Shibuya, one of the trendy parts of Tokyo and only ten minutes by train from our station. So off we went, map in hand, on our first adventure. We felt like Hansel and Gretel walking off to God knows where, with only a vague hope of being able to find our way back. At the station we hit our first hurdle: *kanji,* the Chinese characters that make up the majority of the Japanese writing system. There are only about 50,000 of them. Everywhere we looked it was wall-to-wall *kanji,* and we had no idea what buttons to press or what money to use.

We noticed the train timetable. In the top right-hand corner, in English, was written 'for Shibuya'. Next to it were two or three *kanji.* We figured they must say the same. We tried to memorize their shape, then run to the map, which had all the station names and prices on it, and try to find the same *kanji.* However, a combination of forgetting the *kanji* and being faced with a huge map covered with the squiggles meant that it took us about five round-trip dashes to identify the correct station. All the time the station master kept his eye on us, thinking the *gaijin* equivalent of a pair of headless chickens were trying to overrun his station. We had initially asked him for help but he merely made a cross sign with his hands and in a very heavy accent said, 'NO ENGRISH... NO

ENGRISH!' (The Japanese, it would turn out, have an incessant need to make an X shape with their hands every time they wish to say no. Instead of using *'ie'*, which means 'no', they *avoid* being rude by placing their hands in front of you and ignoring anything else you may say. It's quite effective.)

Eventually we located our train and alighted after precisely ten minutes as Jafar had instructed, all the time making note of the train number, size, colour and any other distinguishing feature or landmark we could find – the visual equivalent of breadcrumbs – and fortunately found ourselves in Shibuya. A quick stroll around the bus stop, hardly the trendiest of places, onto the next train back and to the relative safety of our cubbyhole. Was this it? Six months earlier I had been at university, grown and flourished during my time there, and become unstoppable in my conviction and confidence. But now, even with Jen at my side, I couldn't manage a ten-minute train journey to Shibuya, and I missed my mother.

As the jet lag wore off and the culture shock faded we tried to venture a little farther. Tokyo's subway system sprawled from Yokohama to Chiba, but we figured as long as we got back on to the green Yamanote line, we could find Shibuya and be safe. So we spent a week of getting at first frighteningly, and later pleasantly, lost in Tokyo. By week two we were finally forced to do some work. Jen and I were assigned to different schools, and the first day we stood on the train platform in our crisp new suits and shiny shoes I felt like a child on the first day of school refusing to let go of its mother's hand. We had coped with so much: getting lost, not understanding a word that was said to us, and experiencing racism for the first time. The trains came and took us our separate ways.

They paid us reasonably well at Navo, and the standard six-hour day was hardly taxing. I'd worked as a trainee teacher in a high school before coming to Japan, so I thought I knew what to expect. The Navo people, though, didn't get much above the level we'd already encountered in our housemates. Most of the teachers seemed to exhibit certain abnormalities, and I had a sneaking suspicion that their problems were genetic. Some of the students were no better. I was let into the Navo secret very early on. Clients, not students, are lulled in with far-from-subtle advertisement campaigns. By preying on the insecurity of the Japanese and reinforcing their inability to communicate to the outside world, resulting in misunderstandings, international isolationism and world wars, Navo played up the trendiness of being bilingual and attracted new clients in their droves. They were then sold the idea that their achievable level of English fluency is directly proportional to the amount of money they pay. After a few weeks, students realize that they actually have to study the language to become proficient and many drop out (Navo depends on 70 per cent quitting otherwise the school wouldn't have enough teachers for the lessons required), and most of the remaining clients complete their lessons reluctantly, often not studying and taking their frustration out on the teacher. It wasn't a happy workplace.

We did manage to make friends. Fortunately for us, working in separate schools, we had double the people to choose from. Jen and I joined forces and were able to get to know a decent amount of normal people, who took us under their wings and showed us the sights. Things were starting to look up. I began to realize that living in Japan induced bipolarity, as in the first week I was up and down more times than a five-year-old's yo-yo. From bright, happy mornings to dark, depressing, overcast evenings, it was like the weather in Scotland. I never knew what to prepare for, but as we developed routines and friendships at work, things brightened up and life became easier.

* * *

It had been a month since our arrival in Japan. Culture shock, an incomprehensible train system and having no money meant I still hadn't unpacked my *dogi* (karate suit). All these excuses for not

16

going to the *dojo* were running a bit thin. I was encouraged by Jen.

'When are you going to the *dojo*?'

'Soon,' I would reply, weakly.

My trip with Ishii Sensei all those years ago had irrevocably changed my perception of karate. At home it was a hobby. Here it could literally be a matter of life or death. I had heard that the morning classes were generally the easiest, plus lots of *gaijin* trained then – perhaps there was a correlation. Jen and I had already done a recce, so I knew the lay of the land. The *hombu* (headquarters), which had moved in the five years since I had last had the honour of watching some big guy break a much smaller guy's nose, was at the bottom of a long road, a five-minute-walk from the station. This particularly hot morning at the beginning of August had all the signs of being a killer (people really do die through heat exhaustion in Japan). As I came up from the air-conditioned subway, the humidity hit me like when you take the lid off a steaming pan but forget to stand back first. I could feel my eyebrows singeing. Was this really the day to start? After all, I have a year. What's one more week?

In front of me, walking down the long street, was a young Japanese guy. He looked to be of university age, had a crew cut and unquestionably the biggest calf muscles I had ever seen. He was carrying a rucksack and I knew he was going to the *dojo*. He also looked like he ate *gaijin* for breakfast. A torrent of thoughts ran through my head. Will anyone speak English? Will I be allowed to train? If I am allowed, will it just be so they can kill me? Am I good enough? Last time I trained in Japan I felt protected by Ishii Sensei, but now I was alone.

At sixteen I remember travelling to Ishii Sensei's house in Shropshire to train on one of his notoriously hard black- and brown-belt courses. You had to be sixteen and a brown belt to participate, and I had become both just a month earlier. We slept in his house and trained in the function room above his local pub. Late on

17

the Saturday night some of the senior instructors returning from a night out looking for a space on the floor to sleep. I had nabbed a good spot.

'Who's he?' I heard one say.

'Oh, he's just the little boy from York,' another had commented. From then on, no matter what I achieved, I had always felt that I was just the little boy from York. I shouldn't be in Japan.

The gorilla reached the *dojo* and made a sharp left turn to the entrance. I followed, and was confronted by an empty reception area.

'*Sumimasen.*' I'd practised the conversation a million times over the last couple of weeks, mostly in my sleep. An elderly gentleman in a sharply pressed shirt with a white T-shirt underneath popped his head round the corner and headed over to me.

'*Sumimasen... Eh... Watashi wa... Karate... Urrrm...*'

'Can I help you?'

I looked on in surprise, quickly followed by relief and then the urge to kiss him, but fortunately I managed to regain my composure.

'I would like to train. Is that OK?'

'Of course. Please fill this in.' Forms were quickly handed over.

'And you need to pay this deposit.' A sizeable sum was, with even greater speed and efficiency, taken from me. I was directed to the changing rooms, where a couple of coloured belts and a weedy looking black belt were getting changed. I gave my best bow and got changed myself. I noticed the young Japanese guy from the street was nowhere to be seen... perhaps they had a special cage for him. Fear was building up inside, like some sort of determined fart forcing its way out when you're in polite company, when trying to ignore it only seems to make it worse.

A couple of people, having changed, went into the *dojo*, and as the door opened I tried to get a glimpse of what lay on the other side. I figured if I saw blood-stained walls I could still make a run for it. I also tried to see who would be the *sensei*: maybe the world-renowned Kabe Sensei, known for his lightning-fast back fist and his ability to evade any attack thrown at him. Or maybe it would be Yumoto Sensei, who had been world champion an unprecedented number of times and had feet that suction-gripped the floor. It could also be Takahashi Sensei, the current world champion, who was so fast it defied belief, or Taguchi Sensei, the chief instructor of the Japan Karate Shotorenmei (JKS). He had been training for over fifty years, had gained ninth-degree black belt and even though he was well into his sixties, he had amazing speed, strength and timing, and could easily trounce the young instructors such as Takahashi Sensei.

But the question that was churning my stomach the most was how they would react to me, a *gaijin*. I hadn't seen any other foreigner. I could speak hardly any Japanese, and the little I could speak was useless in the *dojo*, unless they wanted me to order them a beer. I changed, took a deep breath and went in. Ten or so people were practising on their own, waiting for the class to start. With relief I noticed the only other black belt was the Mr Puniverse I had seen in the changing room. I spotted the gorilla in the corner, with a white belt on. No problem – but then I remembered that university students often wore white belts until they got their black belts. In most *dojo* around the world, as *karate-ka* progress through the ranks they wear increasingly darker-coloured belts. Historically, *karate-ka* used to wash their *dogi* but not their belt, so a black belt was held by someone who had simply been training for many years (i.e. it was very dirty). The colour transition in modern *dojo* represented this. But universities hadn't adopted this modern representation of rank and kept to the old system, so Mr Gorilla could well be getting in a little extra training at the *hombu*, in preparation for his black belt in the coming weeks. I watched, waiting for him to do something. He got into stance, ready to perform a front kick, which he did. And thank God – he was crap.

Suddenly I heard a door open and close.

'*Seiritsu!*' Mr Puniverse shrilled out something in Japanese before I had a chance to look around. Everyone rushed to line up. I found my place as a tall figure with dark hair walked to the front and kneeled before the shrine, his back to us. Again Mr Puniverse shouted out further commands and everyone knelt down and bowed to the shrine. I clumsily followed suit, but all I could think was,'Who the hell is he?' Whoever it was, he was tall and, by the way he held himself, he looked deadly.

As I came up from the bow, the *sensei* turned around. He was a foreigner! Before I had a chance to take a reality check we were all bowing again, this time to the *gaijin* sitting at the front. When the formalities finished he spotted me – not difficult, being the only white face in the line-up.

'Hello,' he said in a very educated English accent.

'Urr... *Osu!*' Was that the right response? The word is made up of two characters, the first is 'push', the second is 'spirit' or 'endurance'. *Osu* is used constantly in karate circles to mean yes, no, hello, goodbye, I'm sorry, I'm okay, I understand, I don't understand... The meaning is very contextually based. He looked down at my belt and read the Japanese characters, which I had been led to believe spelt my name.

'Where are you from, Scott?'

'England, *sensei.*' This was amazing, I had come six thousand miles to train at the centre of the karate universe and experience all things Japanese, and on my first day of the adventure I was greeted by a friendly English face.

'Nice to have you here.' This wasn't the nightmare I had envisioned.

Richard Amos Sensei was one of the four foreigners to have completed the instructors' course. I hadn't known much about him beforehand, but I quickly realized that he was one of the best instructors at the *dojo*. His karate was amazing. He executed techniques as if his body were a piece of steel, which had been pulled back until it was about to break and then released to catapult forward with devastating speed and power. It was the very first time I realized that the Japanese didn't have a monopoly on perfect technique – they only have a monopoly on the training techniques that give you the perfect technique. The training was also cool. Not only because the air conditioning was turned on, but also because Richard Sensei's teaching style was laid back, relaxed and informative. We simply practised stepping forward and punching. Trying to spring forward and focus the entire body for the briefest of moments and then relaxing immediately afterwards was so basic, but incredibly difficult. It was a far cry from the lessons I used to have at home. All my fear and nervousness disappeared and I instantly regretted not coming to the *dojo* sooner. This was one of the good, sunny days that can often be found in Tokyo.

* * *

Over the next six months I went from strength to strength. I trained with all the *hombu dojo sensei*. They got to know me and often took time to correct my various bad habits. I quickly got into the routine of training in the mornings and then going to Navo in the afternoons. The morning classes were ideal for getting good tuition because numbers were small and the instructors had time to spend on the students. We would always do the three elements of karate: *kihon, kumite* and *kata*. Known at the three Ks of karate, *kihon* is the practice of basic technique, *kumite* is the sparring element of karate and *kata* is a set pattern of moves where you defend against imaginary opponents: a bit like *Call of Duty* without the need for an Xbox.

I had progressed from dreading the moment I had to enter the *dojo* to skipping down the street, happily anticipating another training session. In karate this just isn't good. Over the years I have come to believe that karate is one of the few hobbies you aren't supposed to enjoy. People have always asked me why I do karate, and before I moved to Japan I fobbed them off by saying I wanted to be like Bruce Lee. Every new student at Navo would

21

ask me why I came to Japan. Students would expect teachers to say something about travel and experiencing new cultures. which they took to mean easy money and beautiful women. But when I said karate, it would often start a discussion as to why I began such a traditionally Japanese art so far away in *gaijin* world, so I had to start thinking of a more accurate answer. My eventual conclusion was that I do karate because it makes the rest of life easy. That is to say, karate training, if done properly, is tough: it's hard work, with little reward because your *sensei* never compliments you. As a result the rest of life, by comparison, becomes easier. I remember when I was eighteen and my friends and I were taking our A levels and everyone was in a perpetual state of panic. I, on the other hand, was fretting about taking my *shodan* (first degree black belt) at about the same time. I had no idea what I would have to face, and the pressure was enormous. However, once I took the grading and passed, it was like some cathartic release, after which A-level exam pressure seemed to have little effect. While my friends were having anxiety induced hissy fits, all I could think was, what's their problem? I have to go to the *dojo* tonight and I'll probably be beaten up. This way of thinking percolated throughout my life. I remember waiting to enter the sports hall for the very last exam of my university finals one sunny Monday morning. I was sitting, hands in my head, when a friend approached.

'Don't worry, it won't be that bad,' he said, trying to cajole me away from despair.

'It's not that,' I reassured him. 'I was in Scotland all weekend, training. I only got back at 2 am.'

So as I found myself skipping to the *dojo*, alarm bells started ringing inside. Too easy... too easy...

I began going to the Saturday night training sessions. These, I had been told, were blood baths, when all the big guns, the *sempai* (seniors) of the *dojo*, came out to play. It was a perfect symbiosis of Japanese culture: *kohai* (juniors, or wannabe *sempai*) dragged themselves to training and to facilitate their relocation to the higher ranks, *sempai* beat them into submission. Every evening's training had the same pattern: basic technique drills quickly followed by sparring. The drills were no different from the *kumite* we did in the mornings. We were given a simple one-two combination we had to attack with and our partners would block and counter. Nothing special there. But the atmosphere in the Saturday sessions was different. The adrenaline and electricity in the air were almost tangible and I knew if I switched off for a split second I would end up paying dearly for it.

I learnt this lesson fast. On my first night, after about ten minutes, I let my concentration wander. I was paired up with Tamata Sempai at the time. He attacked with the prescribed one-two combination, but my defences were lacking, and it only took the tiniest of moments – thinking of who I was going to meet for a beer after training – to end up on the floor, bleeding from the mouth. I felt foolish, like an amateur in the big league. I jumped up, wiped the blood on my sleeve and started again, determined to not let it happen twice. Of course, it happened on many occasions. Saturday evenings scared the hell out of me, but I always survived. Ideally, I could train in the mornings and improve my technique and then train on Saturday and see if my perceived improvement worked under pressure.

By December things were looking good. I had started to study Japanese, and although progress was slow, it was a start. Jen and I had explored most of Tokyo and Shibuya, only ten short minutes away, was a hub of activity, and our weekends were often spent there. Training was going well too. The instructors were friendly and treated me with respect. I also felt I was getting stronger. In the second week of December we had a headquarters competition, where all members could fight it out for top-dog position. Most of the *sempai* refereed, so I was more than happy to enter, and, surprisingly, I won. For the first time in a long while I felt I was no longer in emotional free fall. Life was predictable. I went training, then work and then home, with the odd excursion to the pub. It couldn't get any better.

Of course it was too easy.

'What are we doing here?' It was a general question with a specific meaning.

'Working... karate... drinking...' I tried to weasel my way out of this tricky situation. Jen never really took to Japan like I did. We both, at times, struggled with the racism, but Jen had the added ingredient of sexism to deal with. She was a curvy, blonde, beautiful westerner who was the constant victim of unwanted attention from businessmen. Japan is a safe country but it does have a problem with sexual crime. A high percentage of rape goes unreported and women are forever being touched on crowded trains. The problem is so bad that Japan Rail have women-only carriages during rush hour. It was a lot for Jen to deal with.

'If I am putting up with this hell because of you, you have to goddamn make sure you are making the most of it!'

I was told in no uncertain terms that I had to try for the instructors' course, which had been my secret desire all along; I couldn't turn back now.

Of course you can't simply go up and ask to be allowed on the course. Things have to be done subtly. Candidates have to wait to be invited on the course by the instructors, so my only hope was to put myself in a position to be able do the course, and hope someone would notice.

I set out to be noticed. One morning, after training with Richard Sensei, I cornered him in reception.

'*Sensei*, hope you don't mind me asking, but...'

'Of course not. What is it?' He was like James Bond, suave but deadly.

'I would really like to train more, but, you know, with Navo...' Navo was really putting the brakes on my training schedule. Like my housemates, I was starting to become one of those 'Oh my God, I've just had to work six hours' type of teachers.

'Easy! Quit Navo and start the instructors' course. Do you want to take the test?'

Of course I did. Within days it was decided that I should try out for the test in April and I could start straight away. In eight months I had gone from a lost child wandering around the streets of Tokyo to a potential candidate for the most revered karate course in the world. I was back! There would be no stopping me now!

But there was. Mark, my best friend at university and vice-captain of the karate club, which we had run together. In March he came to Japan for three weeks, and on his second night in Tokyo we hit the clubs in Shibuya, dazzling everyone with our cool dancing. After having tasted every regional sake from around the country, Mark and I decided to climb onto the stage. Unfortunately the party was cut short when I fell off – Mark pushed me – and landed badly in a very intoxicated heap on the floor. The next morning, as my hangover cleared, I realized my left knee was somewhat bigger than usual. In fact, it was huge. I stupidly thought it would clear up by itself, but after a few days of intense pain, Jen frogmarched me to the doctor.

What followed is too tedious to write about and too painful to try to remember, but in brief I was told that nothing was wrong, although my knee seemed to be saying something completely different. After a few months the swelling went down and I was told I could return to the *dojo*. Five minutes into the session my knee buckled beneath me, and this was followed by three more months of incredible pain. The instructors' course test came and went, and no one could give me an answer, other than there was nothing wrong. I was getting a little miffed as it had been five months since the initial accident. At around this time Jen needed to return to the UK to continue her studies, so in July 1998 we packed up and I hobbled to the airport. As soon as I arrived home, I met one of the best orthopaedic surgeons in the country. He looked over my MRI scan, said I had snapped my anterior cruciate ligament and told me that I would never do karate again.

Chapter Two:

Coming Home

Before my injury I was cocksure and borderline egotistical. The belief in myself that I had 'cultivated' at university had only been compounded by my small success in Japan. As European champion, all my self-esteem, the qualities that I thought made me special, came from karate. I would use my little talent in every social situation I faced, finding a way to place myself above everyone else – let's just say that I could, at times, be a bit of an arse. But without my social crutch I quickly deteriorated into depression. My jokes were no longer funny. My friends no longer found me interesting. Without the constant support of Jen, I would have found it all too much. I began to question why I wanted to do karate, and found that, for the first time in my life, I now had a choice (I couldn't even remember starting martial arts at five, it was just something I had always done). Was this really what I wanted to do?

Of course the answer was yes. In the event, I didn't need an operation, but I would have to spend the next nine months doing very painful and time-consuming physiotherapy: and as I was reminded on numerous occasions, it was, obviously, my own fault. I was transformed during those nine months. I rehabilitated hard during my time in the UK, and in February 1999 I was ready to get back to Japan. Without an ounce of my former arrogance to weigh me down and no money for an expensive JAL ticket, I stepped onto an Aeroflot twin-engine cargo carrier, bound for first Moscow and then Japan. On that long journey I began to feel at one with my Aeroflot plane. We both looked and felt old, neglected and were possibly unstable. After eighteen hours, and the start of a nervous twitch under my left eye that stayed with me for two months, we landed in Tokyo. I had no job, no apartment, and no idea if my knee would stand up to training. I was alone in Japan.

Those first few days were desperate. I had booked myself into a cheap *ryokan* in Ikebukuro, an area I knew nothing about. A *ryokan* is a Japanese-style inn, kind of like *Shogun* meets *Fawlty Towers*. I remember lying on my futon feeling an emotional hurricane brewing up inside my gut. Relieved that I was finally back to where I belonged, but at the same time incredibly lonely, I had traded one emotional roller coaster for another. Being back in Japan truly felt like coming home. I had about £3000 left in my Japanese bank account, and to have access to that money, to be independent again (nine months of living with my parents was great motivation to get back to fitness) and to see some of my Japanese friends again was what my life was supposed to be like.

Being away from Jen and going to places that we had explored together, counting down the hours before I could call her again, was causing me near-physical pain. The first few nights when I was alone in my small room were the hardest. I hadn't met up with any of my friends and as I lay on my futon with a weak light barely illuminating her photographs, it took all my strength to resist running out and calling her from the phone box. I called three or four times a day in the first week and it was the only time I could breathe properly. To hear her voice was an anaesthetic to all the stress and fear that was driving me demented. I struggled to hold it together.

Things got better. When we were at university Jen had spent a year studying in Germany, and we had found a rhythm of sending letters, calling a couple of times a week and counting down the days until we could next meet. This proved good practice for the situation in which we now found ourselves, and we settled easily into a long-distance relationship. After a few days, old friends got back in touch and before I knew it, those dark evenings were replaced by bars, clubs and alcohol-assisted amnesia.

Within a week I had found an apartment, the *dojo* (which had moved again) and a job. My apartment was great. The rent was four hundred pounds a month. It was something an estate agent would call 'bijou', consisting of a three-by-four-metre space. The bedroom held a futon and a small coffee table. The living/dining room was the same room with the futon stored in a crawl-in closet of the type much loved by the Japanese. The kitchen and dining area were conveniently close. To access my combined toaster/microwave/sink all I had to do was lean forward... the ultimate in ergonomics.

The reason I chose this place – as if the above plus points weren't enough – is that I didn't need a *houshonin*. This is an older, wealthier Japanese man (never a woman) who would guarantee to cover all costs, were I to run off with the valuable turn-of-the-century fridge. Without a *houshonin*, I was an outcast in the world of real estate and as such had very little choice of where I could live. So it was that I found myself in a little cubbyhole, which along with nine other cubbyholes made up the impressive apartment complex of Oak House, located in Eidan Akatsuka, northern Tokyo.

As I had to share shower and bathroom facilities I soon became acquainted with a steady stream of fellow residents. Most people don't have a *houshonin* because they have either just arrived in the country (in which case they quickly find a job and move on) or are illegal immigrants. My little abode was mainly filled with the latter. I got to know virtually no one in the three and a half years I was there. It was as if the block was occupied by America's most wanted, continually on the move to prevent detection.

I did get to know James, an Australian who had initially come to Japan on a working-holiday visa. That expired about a week after I moved in, so he spent the rest of the time I knew him leaving the country every three months, then coming back in on a tourist visa. Of course these only last three months, so ninety days later off he would go again, hoping on his return the immigration official wouldn't check the pages and pages of little Japanese stamps he had in his passport and refuse entry. He was studying tae kwon do. The problem is, tae kwon do is from Korea, so he was about a thousand miles east of where he should have been. Coming to Japan to study tae kwon do is like going to France to study Morris dancing. To give him his due, he did want to make it to Korea once he had figured out that Honshu, the largest of the four main islands of Japan, wasn't the Korean peninsula; the only problem was that he was trapped in the purgatory of the Japanese underworld. As an illegal immigrant he could hardly get the best jobs on offer, and he didn't have a university degree, which is usually a necessity for Japanese companies. Consequently every penny James earned was put into a special jar, labelled 'plane ticket fund', which was emptied every three months so he could nip abroad, but he never seemed to have enough money to be able to move over to Korea permanently, and thus found himself in a vicious little circle. For all I know he is still there.

I, on the other hand, settled in and started teaching privately in my new classroom, that is, the coffee table in my room. As I lived near two train lines and was an ex-Navo and qualified English high-school teacher I quickly built up a respectable number of students. It also helped that I was located ten minutes north of Ikebukuro. Ikebukuro is a major station of the Yamanote line, the circle line of Tokyo. Everything inside the green line is considered Tokyo proper and everything outside is the suburbs. This isn't entirely true. The Yamanote line is like the heart of Tokyo that has been rolled out to make a long sausage-shaped corridor of city. At virtually every station along the line you find centres for commerce, culture and shopping. It is true that inside the line there are city-like areas, but for me the stops on the Yamanote line were all you needed.

Locating just north of Ikebukuro was perfect for both work and play.

After about ten days I summoned the courage to try out my new knee at the *dojo*. It had been a year since I had trained with them, and during the long walk from the station, which, due to the relocation, had been extended by a good ten-minute saunter, my mind was working overtime. Would they recognize me? Did they remember I had been injured? Would they take it easy on me until I got completely back to fitness, or would they beat me up and ruin my knee for ever? To my surprise they remembered and welcomed me back with open arms (as much as the Japanese can). I wasn't given any special considerations, but I managed the training and the more sessions I survived the stronger I felt. I now had to wear a hinged knee support, and had brought two with me. The larger one went from below my calf to above my thigh. Strapped tight, it prevented any 'slippage' and after a few drills from the *sensei* it became soaked in sweat and very heavy. Nervous and unsure, I began using the smaller support, which offered less support. This was fine for basic drills and *kata*, but it was the unpredictability of *kumite* that scared me. A few times as I stepped back, out of the way of an attack, I got 'slippage'. It was an awful feeling and brought back so many horrible emotions and memories. However, over time I understood how to tense my surrounding muscles to protect my knee and prevent further damage.

In those first couple of months I thrived in my new lifestyle and came to love living in Eidan Akatsuka.

I often thought that Tokyo wasn't just one city. The place is enormous, but it felt as if it were made up of a patchwork of cities, towns and villages. Eidan Akatsuka was definitely a village, where life seemed slower compared to the hustle and bustle of Yamanote-line Tokyo.

I became fully acquainted with the slower pace of life on my first-ever trip to a proper Japanese barber. By this point I had already spent over a year in Japan, but whilst at Navo, in a bid

31

to save money – one of Jen's more endearing qualities was to be constantly putting us on economy drives – I always had to use the station barber. This guy had a small Portaloo outside the local station where you queued up outside until it was your turn, went in, got a short back and sides (no matter what you asked for) and he then actually vacuumed your head to get rid of all loose hair and sent you on your way. Cheap and cheerful.

I had heard that a real Japanese barber can be a treat, so off I went to find my village barber. It was easily spotted as he still had the twirling red and white swizzle-stick sign out front, and as I entered the shop I walked into an age long forgotten back home. I was ushered to a luxurious leather seat that had a 1920s Chicago feel to it, and the process of my embalmment began. First a length of tissue paper was wrapped around my neck, then two immaculately clean, perfectly ironed 'barber capes' – an inner then an outer cape – were placed over me. Each time my barber took great care to get a snug fit by using his finger to gauge whether he was cutting off the oxygen supply to my head. Finally I was capped off with a heavy, lead-weighted scarf, which had the effect of keeping everything perfectly in place. After ten minutes prep we were ready to start. My Japanese was improving, but when learning a language you start to realize you have gaping holes in your ability. I had never learned nor attempted to use 'barber Japanese', and as I sat there, trying to explain what I wanted, I had terrible visions of what the misinterpretation and result could be. A reassuring and knowing smile came across my new friend's face, and off we went.

I always have my hair short. I find it gives me that look of hardness at which the rest of my features fail miserably. So the first thing I always expect is the clippers, but Japan's answer to Vidal Sassoon never once reached for them and just snipped away, follicle by follicle, strand by strand. I had been told, whilst at Navo, that western barbers cut hair like we mow a lawn, whilst Japanese barbers cut hair like pruning a Bonsai tree. I thought it had merely been the ranting of one of the many racist students, but now I was beginning to see he had a point. Slowly Mr Sassoon worked his way around my head, clipping and scissoring like a great artist immersed in his work. An hour or so later he reached for the mirror, beamed with pride, and showed me the back. I offered my thanks and was about to stand up when he nipped around the front and started fumbling with the mirror/shelf/scissor-holding unit that had been in front of me all the time. With a flick of the switch the unit sprouted a wash basin, shampoo, conditioner and fresh-smelling white towels. The whole contraption was like some child's Transformer toy. Mr S. had again nipped back behind me and was now pushing me forward into the torrent of water. With the energy of a kamikaze pilot he scrubbed and invigoratingly attacked every strand on my head.

After a quick rub down, which included an excursion up my nostrils and down my ears, I was flung back to find that the chair had now been moved to a horizontal position. I caught a glimpse of the clock and realized I had been there nearly an hour and a half, before a very hot, wet towel was placed on my face. As I steamed away, I heard the sharpening of a blade next to my right ear, and without warning, the towel was whipped off, I was lathered up and Mr S. proceeded to give me the closest shave I had ever had. Nothing was spared from his cut-throat: not my sideburns, not the back of my neck, not even my eyebrows, which, for the first time since puberty, had form again. He even shaved my ears. You never know what a jungle there is back there, until someone takes a machete to them.

I felt my pruning had finished and as he took off my cocoon, I was amazed to find that *not a single hair* had escaped southwards to irritate the hell out of me for the rest of the day – one of my pet hates. I was just about to thank him for his time, effort and mastery with everything sharp, when he reached for a bottle of green liquid. With a vigorous shake, my head was covered by this menthol-smelling rub, and he started to give me a head massage that bordered on the sublime. Every pressure point and stressed-out area was worked on. But he didn't stop there. He worked down, relaxed my neck, grabbed my chin and gave my head a twist, making several of those clicking sounds that you get when you visit a chiropractor after a major car accident. Then the other way; crack, crack, crack. My body had never felt so good in all the years I'd had it. Next he moved onto my shoulders, arms and then hands, and as he massaged, he cracked each individual knuckle of every finger on both hands. I hadn't known that was even possible, but my body felt fantastic. I look at the clock, realizing I had been with Mr S. for nearly two hours, and the end must be near. As I was half asleep by this point he gave me a quick blow-dry and put my hair in a perfect setting, gave me a little brush down and walked away, presumably to allow me to recover. Ten seconds later he returned, took the seat next to me, and, with a look of 'was it good for you?' offered me a cigarette, and lit one himself.

I couldn't believe it. I had to refuse the post-coital pleasure (I don't smoke), and I often wonder if he felt betrayed by my rejection after all we had been through. It was such great service for only £10 or so. From then on I always went to Mr S. for my haircut, and the service never changed, although I suspect he always harboured a wish for me to take up smoking, so we could both truly share the whole cutting experience together.

The rest of Eidan Akatsuka was equally interesting. Instead of family run bakeries we had family run sushi shops, the local bowling green was replaced by a judo *dojo* where a seventy-year-old master hurled people through the air on a nightly basis, and the local pub was replaced by a hostess club where tired *sararimen* returning from work in the city could wind down and relax whilst ageing hostesses poured them drinks. *Sarariman,* a corruption of "man who receives a salary", are the workforce behind Japan's success. They pour into the city early in the morning and stagger out to the suburbs late at night.

We also had our many different family run shops, which were

always named after the owner. Suzuki Sushi, Fujiyama Fashion and Terimoto Tyres spring to mind. The problem was that they wanted to be trendy, so signs in English were the way to go. Unfortunately your average shop owner in the little villages of Tokyo has limited grasp of anything English. The local hardware store, owned by Mr Yoshida, suffered greatly from English ignorance. The sign-makers obviously had no idea about capital and small-case lettering in English, so his sign read 'YosHiDA hARdwArE'. Underneath Mr Yoshida had wanted to give his customers a creed by which to live. 'Be who you are!' was obviously the message he wanted to convey. However, as we know the English love to contract their language, therefore it came out as 'Be wHO yOu'rE'. This was then followed by a message to younger customers. In the window was a picture of a cuddly teddy bear with a speech bubble coming out of his mouth. With an arm pointing away from the door he was telling all children to 'FuCk ofF'.

I'm sure Mr YosHiDA had no idea of the mistakes and meanings of his little signs, and with the entertainment I got from it every time I passed by, I wasn't about to put him straight.

Eidan Akatsuka had everything I needed: idiosyncratic shop owners, geriatric hostesses and even a sports centre. The whole of Tokyo is split into wards, with each ward having to provide facilities for its residences at a much-reduced fee. Being a resident and having plenty of free time I enrolled at the local gym thinking I would supplement my karate training with stamina work and a few weights, plus it was always good to meet new local people. So on my first trip there, one Wednesday afternoon, I was pleased to find an assortment of students, housewives and pensioners cycling, rowing and stepping away on the various cardiovascular machines. I mounted one of the step machines and started climbing the virtual equivalent of the Empire State Building. An elderly gent to my left, realizing a *gaijin* was in his orbit, started to take a keen interest in me. It was probably the first time he had seen a foreigner and I could see him building up the courage to start talking to me.

'Hello. Do you speak Japanese?'

'Yes, I do... How very nice to meet you.' My Japanese was so formal.

'Oh, very good. I'm seventy-two.'

It has always amazed me that in the west, when old people reach a certain age, the fact that they are still alive becomes the most important thing to them, their best achievement, and everything else is relegated to a very poor second. They then feel duty-bound to inform all. I was delighted to find the same was also true in Japan.

The septuagenarian looked like Mr Magoo. He took great delight in telling me how he came to the gym every afternoon to keep his ticker going, and I took great delight in watching his mole-like eyes trying to follow me as I bobbed up and down, progressing up the Empire State. I then had about twenty minutes of the usual Japanese-meeting-a-gaijin-for-the-first-time type conversation: Are you American? Where else could you possibly be from? Can you use chopsticks? After Mr Magoo was satisfied with his information, he made his excuses and bounced off, like a human pinball machine, to the more sedentary massage chair.

I carried on with my workout, failed miserably at trying to give the glad eye to a couple of cute Japanese university students, and finished my session about an hour later. As I entered the changing rooms I spotted Mr Magoo getting changed next to the showers. He was so pleased to see me again and we chatted away as I stripped off to take a shower, but when I took off my trousers he stopped mid-syllable, pointed and said, '*Ookii*' – big. Now, in Japanese there are no plurals and no definite articles, so *Ookii* could have meant 'it is big' or 'they are big'. It is such a contextually based language that when something is said out of the blue, its meaning can be a somewhat ambiguous.

As I walked to the shower, he continued to point and refer to the largeness of something. My thighs, perhaps? After all I had just been working out. It was when I reached the entrance to the shower he stopped me, and with both hands grabbed my dick. (Actually, I can't get away with that. He only used one hand, gave it a good tug and remarked on its size and how in all his seventy-two years he had never seen such a big one, whilst all the while getting up close and giving it a good look.)

I have often heard people talk of out-of-body experiences. Well, I had one. I looked down, thinking, for what seemed like an eternity, that this wasn't happening, that this couldn't be happening. Eventually, with the force of being thrust back into my body at high speed, I pushed his hand away and stammered, 'This essentially means bad, naughty, not a good thing. It's the closest the Japanese can get to saying fuck off. That's why they have such difficulty understanding the significance of swear words – they have no frame of reference. *Yo* adds extra feeling and roughly translated, means 'you know'. In Japanese, that's as strong as it gets.

With an 'Oh, OK,' he carried on getting changed and talking about how next year he would be seventy-three. I scurried into the shower and after trying to cleanse myself of the experience by washing four times, returned to the locker room to find him fully dressed, ready to go, and just waiting to say goodbye. With politeness only the Japanese can get away with, he wished me luck, said he hoped to see me again, and was gone. To this day, I still don't think there was any sexual motivation behind his violation, much to my friends' gasps of disbelief. After all this is a country where men encourage friends by patting each other on the bum and where women publicly grab each other's breasts to judge size, shape and firmness. To be on the safe side, though, I never went back to the gym in the afternoons again.

During those months life seemed to be swimming along nicely and by April it was full steam ahead. Nothing had been mentioned about the instructors' course, but I was already too late for the 1999 course and so had a whole year to make my political connections and manoeuvres in order to be in the right place at the right time. I also had to decide whether I truly wanted to do the course.

I still harboured ideas of just doing a year or so of hard training at the *hombu*, and making do with that. However, in the second week of April something happened that changed everything. Six weeks after I had arrived back a letter from Jen arrived in the post. We had been together nearly six years, but in those six weeks of separation she had decided that this lifestyle, and the life we had planned for each other, wasn't what she had signed up for. She wanted out. I thought I would give her the dignity of being able to say it to my face, so I flew home with Virgin Atlantic – these types of emergencies call for travelling in style. But Jen never really gave me a satisfactory answer. She married three months later, eloping to Gretna Green.

A week later, emotionally exhausted, I returned to Japan. Now I was truly determined. Before, I had questioned joining the instructors' course. I wanted to be with Jen and two years on the course would have kept me from her. I still desperately wanted to be with her. That wasn't possible now, so my excuse of not doing the course was gone. I decided if the best relationship I had ever had was going to be sacrificed for karate, then I had better make sure it was worth it. Once more, I gave it everything.

That whole year was non-stop training and teaching English. I was lucky to find a number of English students who were willing to study during the day, giving me time to train every evening. My karate form was coming back, and in the summer of 1999 I returned home and won the European Championships again.

Back in Japan I started to make inroads with the junior instructors. Koyama Sensei was in his final year of the instructors' course, and he was also secretly dating Claudia, one of my friends from the dojo, a *nidan* - a second degree black belt - from France. We went out drinking together on numerous occasions and trained with each other three or four times a week. The odd subtle hint here and a word into Claudia's ear there, and by the start of the new millennium I was ready for anything.

Chapter Three:

The Test

The *dojo* has moved again.

Now we are in a brand-new purpose-built facility about twenty minutes from my house. How great is that? I haven't been there before, so as I make my way there, to take the test for the instructors' course, I'm looking forward to seeing the new location. I'm a little worried about what I will have to do for the test. I know it will be one *kata*... no problem... and a little *kumite*. That will be tough, as last week Koyama Sensei gave me a hard time and I'm thinking it was a taster of what's to come. I arrive at *Sugamo* station, and for the very first time I am eagerly strolling the five minutes to the *dojo, dogi* in hand, to begin training. This is it! I have finally made it. The outside of the dojo is beautifully covered with Japanese calligraphy and fronted with a small Japanese garden. I'm going to be part of something great.

I enter the *dojo* and all the *sensei* are there: Taguchi, Yumoto, Shima, Yamada, Takahashi, Koyama and another four I have never seen before. They look tough. I give a deep bow and a friendly smile... a bit of an ice-breaker, never fails. I'm told to change, and as I walk into the locker room I am confronted with a young and fresh-looking lad.

'*Osu.*' I give him a friendly greeting, realizing he is Sueki, my fellow trainee instructor and *doki* – meaning classmate or colleague.

Or simply the only other person in 2000 stupid enough to try out for the course!

'*Osu*,' he grimaces back. I put it down to nerves – after all we're both going to take this test. I shake his hand and he is reciprocating with a two-handed handshake. Now that's what I like to see, a healthy respect for his *sempai*: after all, I am one rank higher and five years his senior.

The panel of examiners is sitting and awaiting our 'performance'. Taguchi and Yumoto Sensei are flanked by the four unknowns. It's a good job I gave them all a smile.

I've done my *kata*. No problems. I didn't get any nods of approval, but Sueki only did *Bassai Dai*, a fairly basic kata, and he wasn't too hot at that.

'Next *kumite*!' Shima Sensei announces with increased enthusiasm. I notice a change of mood in everyone. Taguchi Sensei, who has been looking almost bored until this point, is now looking alert, like a predator on the scent of blood.

Here goes. Sueki. I don't want to give him too much of a hard time, he is my *doki*, after all. What the hell was that? I'm on the floor, and can feel blood trickling down from my nose and building up in my mouth. How could I have been hit in the nose and the mouth at the same time? He must have fists the size of plates. Shima comes over and kicks me. 'Get up! Continue!'

'No, no. I'm injured, there's been some sort of mistake. Sueki hit me without using control. That's not allowed, is it?'

'GET UP!'

I'm already brain damaged, because without saying a word I'm back on my feet, waiting for more. I'm on the floor again. This time I think it was a kick... I hear '*Yame*' - stop. Thank God, it's all over. I struggle to my feet, bow and begin to walk off. As I do, a guttural Japanese voice commands me to stay. I turn round, and I'm facing Koyama Sensei.

'That's okay,' I naively think. 'He's my friend, we drink together.'

WHACK. I'm on the ground again, looking up at Koyama Sensei, hoping my innocent eyes will induce some compassion in him. CRACK! He's just stamped on my head. He actually brought up his foot and slammed my head into the *dojo* floor. I hear '*Yame*' again, and Koyama is replaced by Takahashi. Takahashi is blindingly fast, and all I remember is at one point Shima, who is refereeing this rule-less fight, grabs the back of my *dogi*, preventing me from going head first over the table where Taguchi, Yumoto and the four dignitaries are sitting – who, incidentally, haven't batted an eyelid at the grotesque show of violence taking place in front of them.

Eventually '*Yame*' is called again. I'm virtually dragged to the sidelines, where I watch Sueki do his two blood-free bouts. Why aren't they knocking the living daylights out of him, too? All I can really think is, I've just found hell on earth.

It had all happened so quickly. The owners of the building we were using in 1999 had told the JKS at the beginning of the year that we had to be out by Christmas. So with true Japanese efficiency they started looking for a place in November. Tokyo, one of the most overcrowded cities in the world, is not the best area to find a place fast. So entering the new millennium we were out in the cold with nowhere to train. Luckily I was still able to go to Koyama Sensei's *dojo*, so I could continue training three times a week with him and by February, Yumoto and Takahashi Sensei started holding morning training sessions at a local sports gym near my house. Despite their incompetence, for me it wasn't so bad. In March, Yumoto Sensei announced they had found a venue and that the new *hombu dojo* would be ready for the start of the new academic year in April. This is also when the *kenshusei* or trainee instructor programme starts. As he was walking out of the *dojo*, almost as an afterthought, he turned to me.

'Come to the *dojo* on Friday at 12.'

'*Osu.*' I managed to get in a little bow before he walked off, without any explanation as to why I should turn up, and more importantly where the new *dojo* was. Like always in karate, direct contact between *sensei* and student is kept to a minimum, so I had to rely on my *sempai* to fill in the blanks.

'Congratulations!' Tamata-san was patting me on the back.

'For what?'

'For being invited onto the instructors' course. I have to start calling you *sensei* now.'

That short sentence was my invitation to join the *kenshusei*. Cold shivers run down my spine now when I think of how I carried on my life without any idea of what I was about to let myself in for.

The test was scheduled for 17 March, and I thought I might have time to pop back home for a bit of R&R before I started the course proper. During a training session with Takahashi Sensei I innocently asked him how soon after the test the course was expected to start. He staggered back as if I had just passed wind. 'What?'

'Instructors' course, when start? I maybe go home.' I thought my Japanese had failed me yet again, so I tried to ask a different way. Unfortunately, he had understood completely and as he shoulder-barged past me, he muttered something under his breath that suggested I should be more worried about passing the test than thinking about going home. With hindsight I cringe at my naivety. However, on deeper analysis, my reaction to that first incident with Takahashi Sensei marked the beginning of how I would attempt to deal with the nightmare that lay ahead of me. What could they possibly do? It wasn't as if they could beat me up – that sort of thing was illegal, even in Japan.

At half past twelve on 17 March 2000 I found myself sitting at a desk in front of the panel, finishing the written test. I was still in a state of shock. Blood – my blood – was all around me. On the floor, on the desk, slowly drip, drip, dripping from my chin. My *dogi* was red. In any other country I would have been whisked off to a hospital and the distinguished panel sitting in front of me would have been helping police with their enquiries. On the contrary, I now sat in front of the panel helping them with their enquiries. I had to answer a couple of essay style questions: 'Where does karate come from?' and 'What does karate mean to you?' My hand was shaking as I wrote the answers. I just couldn't stop the physical and emotional exhaustion from taking over my body, and my piece of paper started to look like a spider had trodden in ink and then crawled all over the page. I wanted to answer that the karate these guys did obviously came from hell, and what it meant to me was blood, bruises and fear. My whole conception of karate, fifteen years of experience, had been irrevocably changed but I kept to the party line and talked about karate being an honourable form of self-defence originating in Okinawa 400 years ago, and to me it was a way of improving myself, gaining confidence, self-awareness and a deeper insight into life. This was quite true. I was now fully aware of my nose, left eye and several ribs – and what could give a greater insight into one's life than seeing one's blood all around?

Luckily I was allowed to write my answers in English. The panel could only speak Japanese, so it was decided that I would read out my answers and Koyama Sensei would translate. His English was perfect. The desks had been removed and I sat all alone in front of these guys, my hands still shaking, trying to focus on my spider-crawl handwriting. My jaw had started to seize up, my left eye was already black and blue and I began to resemble E.T. However, phoning home was not an option, so I started with the answers. Koyama was translating so I spoke to him. Big mistake. Yumoto Sensei hit the roof.

'Look at us!' He demanded, and I instantly lost the will to live.

What followed was a thirty-minute, World-War-II-style interrogation. I quickly realized that the written test was just a formality. After I gave them my extensive background knowledge of karate, which at every turn was ripped apart by the four cronies flanking Taguchi and Yumoto, they proceeded with further questioning.

'Why do you want to become *kenshusei*?' fired one.

43

'Do you think you are strong enough?' another asked skeptically.

'What is your connection with Ishii Sensei?' This one just confused me.

I struggled for answers, but like some demented quiz show, I was obviously against the clock and had to come up with coherent, comprehensive answers in ten seconds or less and convince them why I wanted to join their sadistic club. It seems sick to me that they would put me through the worst experience of my life and then ask me to justify why they should allow me to continue.

I would love to be able to report that I made a passionate speech, talking about dreams, destiny and the pursuit of one's true path. Alas, I think my somewhat stuttered answer involved getting stronger, becoming a good fighter and providing them with an easy to hit, moving punch-bag. My time was up. I was dismissed and told to change. I went to the changing room, trying to catch what they were saying to Sueki. It sounded like they were having a tea party. At one point I heard laughter, and imagined Sueki had just cracked a good *gaijin* joke and they were all splitting their sides over it. I couldn't believe the difference between us now. From the moment I walked through the door there was no going back. I had entered the strictest martial arts programme in the world, and they were sure going to let me know about it. With Sueki's 'interrogation' finished, he quickly changed and we were told to follow them to a restaurant. Like a mother duck taking her young for a walk, Taguchi Sensei led the way followed by the four dignitaries, Yumoto, the rest of the junior instructors, Sueki and last and definitely least, me. Arriving at the restaurant, Yumoto Sensei gave us a withering look. 'Go over there!' Sueki and I did as we were told - the Japanese language has no real swear words. Telling someone to 'go over there' is similar to telling them to fuck off!

The Japanese have the most national holidays of any industrialized country, finding really bizarre things to celebrate in order to justify their monthly bank holiday. This day just happened to be one of those holidays, and I knew my friends would be celebrating National Grab-a-Geisha Day. I have often found in moments of stress that beer provides the perfect remedy, so off I went in search of enlightenment. Horrified at my appearance, my *gaijin* friends wanted to call the police, but it was only their complete lack of Japanese language skills that prevented them from doing so. They did try to enlist the help of our Japanese friends.

'What's all the fuss about?' A friend's girlfriend asked.

'That's what happens when you do karate,' another chipped in.

I found myself agreeing with them. My *gaijin* friends looked at me in disbelief. I had always been a normal *gaijin*, fighting the system, fighting the need to speak Japanese, fighting to beat the old granny to the last seat on the train. Now I had been transformed into a *hen na gaijin*, someone who has gone native, pretending to be something he obviously isn't. I was someone who would allow himself to be beaten up, and accept it as normal.

On the way home, my temporary beer-induced numbness dissolved under the scrutiny of Japanese day-trippers who found my battered appearance to be compulsive viewing. I staggered from the train station past the *Koban* - Police Box - only for the policeman to look me in the eyes and retreat quickly back into his hole. I limped into my local *Conbini*, Japan's answer to the convenience store. I rummaged around the newly stocked dinnertime fridge for something to eat. I couldn't face going home to my lonely room yet, so I paced up and down the aisles. It was only small, but due to the international envied *Conbini* stock rotation system all the needs of an evening were available. Toothbrushes would be replaced by caffeine tablets as morning became afternoon and caffeine tablets replaced by condoms as afternoon became night. Tokyo was the most efficient city in the world and I loved living here, but the day's events had taken their toll. I brought my chicken fried rice and toddled home.

I woke the next morning to find that it hadn't all been a dream.

The phone was ringing and on the other end was Koyama Sensei, ringing to give me the 'happy' news that I was in. I had been accepted and the course would start on 3 April.

However, there was a but...

In April 1997 Carlos Martin, a Portuguese *karate-ka*, had attempted and successfully become *kenshusei* – he had only lasted until the autumn before returning home due to family problems. Taguchi and Yumoto Sensei were not happy, although I am sure they felt vindicated, as Carlos proved *gaijin* were just not up for the *kenshusei* programme. But in spring 1998 Carlos returned and pleaded to be let back on the course. He was allowed back, reluctantly, but a year later he was offered a teaching post in Spain and took it. He left the course for a second and final time. Yumoto Sensei swore he would never allow another *gaijin* on the course again – and then I came along.

The Japanese belief that foreigners can't take it is completely unfounded. When Yumoto Sensei started the course, three other Japanese *karate-ka* started with him. He was the only one to complete it. This 75 per cent drop-out rate is quite normal, but with the *gaijin kenshusei* there is a much lower drop-out rate of about 50 per cent. This was simply because the hardships, sacrifices and challenges *gaijin* had to face to even be *asked* onto the course were tremendous. If they did make it that far, they had already proven their worth. History is often written by the victors, and this time it was the Japanese. On top of my being a *gaijin*, my *sensei* back in the UK was not a popular man in Japan. Ishii Sensei, although Japanese, acted more western most of the time. He was direct, honest, upfront and in your face, all the things that the Japanese despise. He also liked drinking and the trappings of a liberal western lifestyle. Within the JKS there were certain elements that wanted to distance themselves from him and I, as his top student, was tarred with the same brush. So despite having trained diligently at the *hombu* for nearly three years, convincing them I wasn't going to leave as soon as it became tough or start bringing shame onto the JKS was a difficult prospect.

A decision was made. I would be allowed on the course but I would not receive the fringe benefits of *kenshusei*, that is, a salary. As well as training daily, *kenshusei* have to do all the administrative and cleaning work at the *dojo*, organize JKS events, teach when instructors were away and basically fulfil every whim of one's *sempai*. The upside, however, is the money: *kenshusei* are taken care of by the JKS and by *sempai*. They don't have to worry about rent, food, transport or holidays. Everything is provided in order for them to concentrate on getting good at karate. I was a risk, as they didn't want to invest time or money into someone who would soon leave or be thrown out. So I received a different deal. I would become *Gaijin Kenshusei*, which would be called *Shugyosei*. This meant 'someone who trained to the extreme'. I would have to do exactly the same as normal *kenshusei* (training, administration, cleaning, organizing) and I would receive the same qualifications, but I would receive no financial aid or support whatsoever from my *sensei/sempai*.

'Do you understand your situation?' My friend, and now *sempai*, was making sure he had made clear the exact nature of the bum deal I was getting.

'Yes, Koyama Sempai, I understand.' I accepted, wondering why they had asked me to try out for the course in the first place. So far I had been beaten up, interrogated and now denied any help. Why not ask me to put one hand behind my back when I was fighting as well? Koyama sempai told me the course would start on at 12 pm on 3 April.

* * *

I had a couple of weeks to relax. It was *hanami* time in Japan, when the whole of Tokyo becomes a sea of pinks and reds as the cherry trees bloom. It is truly a fantastic sight, made even better by the traditional way of celebrating the event. At this time of year the Japanese hold *hanami* parties where large crowds of people go to the park, spread some sheeting under a tree, unpack millions of Tupperware containers, unload several barrels of beer and sake and eat and drink themselves into a stupor. As foreigners it is one of the few times we feel we should respect the culture we have found ourselves in, and follow the traditional way of getting drunk at what amounts to a rather posh picnic. Companies even order their most junior office members to scout out the best locations during the mornings: they are then forced to sit patiently all day protecting their reserved turf, only to be sent home in the evening as their bosses arrive to enjoy a party in the prime location.

Having rearranged most of my evening English classes and still sporting my battle scars, I set off to meet my friends and see how long it would take to lose the ability to focus on all the natural beauty that surrounded us. The main topic of conversation was my gruesomeness and how I had come by it. I explained how they had beaten me up, and people seemed genuinely impressed by the whole affair. I even started believing my own publicity. I assured them that this was just the test and that it wouldn't be happening on a daily, or even weekly, basis. We all laughed. Who could take beatings like this on a weekly basis? Deep down, I knew that this was just the start of it.

April 3, like so many things that you dread coming, arrived quickly. I arrived at the *dojo* at 11.30 am. The lesson started at noon, but the morning class for regular students didn't finish until 11.30 am, so I thought it was good timing. I walked in just as the class was finishing and as I looked up from my bow I saw Yumoto, Takahashi, Yamada, Shima, Koyama and Sueki all looking at me with hatred in their eyes. They had all already done an hour in the morning class. I had broken the first unwritten rule of *kenshusei*, which is always to train in the morning class. I scurried into the changing room and put on my *dogi*. How bad could it be? I had shown I was tough enough, now all they had to do was teach me how to be good. We warmed up and started training. First was *kihon*. We began by standing in front of the mirror and doing fifty punches with each hand and then fifty kicks with each leg. They were amazing, never tiring – they didn't even stop to get their breath back. I had never done anything that approached this level in my life. After the little 'warm up' in front of the mirror, we moved to the back of the *dojo*. Again facing the mirror we started *ido kihon* – stepping *kihon*. Moving forward and back, we drilled several techniques each time; very draining and as boring as hell. I was flanked by Takahashi Sensei and the power he generated with each step was tangible. More importantly, as we continued, he maintained that level of strength. Sets of twenty were completed, followed by a short thirty second break. After an hour we were all drenched in sweat and I could barely stand, but Takahashi Sensei was still producing techniques of such ferocity that I could feel it through the floor.

Kihon was then followed by *kumite* drills, thirty minutes of different combinations with a partner. These were always a one-two combination, the simplicity of which highlights every mistake and forces you to focus on the most efficient way to attack and defend. I was paired up with Takahashi Sempai and yet again he was after blood. I hoped he had seen enough of my particular variety, but again I was deluding myself. Before long my lip was split (in a different place than the previous week) and my eyes were watering due to a rather vicious *mawashi-geri* - roundhouse kick - that caught me square on the nose as I sheepishly turned my head away in fear. Again, none of them seemed to tire. Takahashi Sensei moved with such fluidity and relaxation – this allowed him to sustain his power, but the more nervous I became, the more I tensed up. It was a vicious circle.

Jiyu-kumite - the dangerous freestyle sparring - followed and I found out that Takahashi Sempai wasn't the only bloodthirsty demon in the group. They were all after me. I tried a few things that had worked in the past. The first time I trained in Japan I found that standing my ground when attacked showed I wasn't intimidated. Now standing my ground only increased the force of the impact on my face. Moving about and trying to stay out of the way only fatigued me more quickly and no matter where I moved I couldn't escape the speed of their attacks. I also wasn't used to the type of *kumite* we were doing. I would normally expect to fight with the idea of scoring a point, as we do in competitions, but there were no points to be scored today. They attacked with a one-two combination, often hitting with the second attack. But it didn't stop there. As the distance was reduced, they attacked with an elbow or a knee. When they got even closer they grabbed hold of me and threw me to the ground. I was obviously out of my league. Eventually '*Yame*' was called. I thought that after an hour and forty-five minutes of full-on training we were finished. Wrong. Yumoto Sensei grunted and Sueki and I got up to do one last bout of *jiyu-kumite*. Sueki was looking unbelievably fresh and blood-free as we paired up. I threw out a few things and I like to think that one or two got through, but I was far too tired to really know or care. Then, with speed that is rarely seen outside wildlife programmes, Sueki pounced, sweeping my left leg – and from my injured left knee I felt – and I am sure heard – something crack. I hobbled back and fortunately Yumoto Sensei called it a day.

My first lesson was over, but by the time I got to the shower my knee had started to swell. By the time I arrived home it was the size of a football, looking distinctly like it had when I had first injured it the year before. Panic set in. I went to the physiotherapist to be told I had torn my cartilage. It was impossible to tell how badly, but it looked serious, and I would probably need an operation. One thing was for certain: I wouldn't be doing karate again anytime soon.

Chapter Four:

The Madness Sets In

I am pregnant. I seem to have developed morning sickness. As I walk to the dojo, clean-cut *sararimen* and beautiful office ladies are jumping out of the way as I make a dash to the nearest alley to throw up. My insides feel like they have been sliced and diced by a sushi chef and my legs are literally weak with fear.

I open the door and from the dojo entrance I hear a thump, thump, thump. Quickly I put my shoes on the shelf nearest the exit (for a quick getaway) and I walk in. Shima, Takahashi, Koyama and Sueki are all staring at me. Clichés like 'if looks could kill' take on a whole new meaning. I scurry to the changing rooms and just before I get there I pass Yumoto Sensei knocking lumps out of the *makiwara* - striking post. He pulls his hand away from the pounded straw target and I half expect to see a picture of me pinned to the surface. I give the deepest bow my legs will allow without toppling over.

As before, training begins with an hour of *kihon* and then *kumite* drills. This is quickly followed by *jiyu-kumite*. My first partner is Takahashi Sempai. He wakes me up with a hard punch to the mouth. Spitting blood, I pull myself off the ground and face him again. He feigns a kick and then as hard as he can delivers an *ashi-bari* sweep to my left, injured, leg. I hit the deck with a thud that Yumoto Sensei's *makiwara* would be proud of and I find myself scrambling to my feet for the second time. Maybe he has forgotten I have been off due to an injured knee caused by Sueki's *ashi-bari*. Maybe I should point this out to him. Thud, I am on the ground again. This time the *ashi-bari* was much higher and frighteningly close to my knee.

Partners are changed and I am facing Koyama Sempai. After a few heavy blows to the body and face, he changes tack. Feigning a punch, he moves in with what is by now the familiar *ashi-bari* and I am on my arse again. Feeling like a human yo-yo, I get up and after several more trips south we change partners and I am now facing Sueki. Surely he must remember I have been away injured – after all it was by his doing. But, no, everyone is suffering from amnesia and he sets out trying to drop me like the others, but with slightly less finesse. '*Yame*' is called and after the warm down we line up and kneel in traditional *seiza* seated position while Yumoto Sensei finishes off the lesson. I am not listening to what he is saying as my left knee is ready to explode, but that pain is dwarfed by the desire to scream, 'I am in hell, my *sempai* are trying to kill me and I need to throw up again!'

I was on first-name terms with my physiotherapist. Her name was Aoife. I dined at her house, drank her expensive wine and with her long blonde hair and penetrating blue eyes, she was beautiful enough to wish injury upon oneself. She had cured an unpleasant-sounding click in my right knee the year before and, during the run-up to the start of the course, had given me regular check-ups to make sure I was on top form. When I hobbled to her clinic after that first session she took a long look and said nothing. I felt we had been through a lot together and she knew my body so well – although not as well as I had always hoped for.

'So what do you think?' I asked at the end of the session.

'You know what it is. It's a tear in your cartilage.'

'Well, what do you think... about a month?'

'No,' she laughed. 'Try two months!'

The next day I went off to the *dojo*. Only two weeks before it had been a five-minute stroll from the station. Yesterday it had been a nerve-wrecking shuffle to the unknown. Now it was a twenty minute pain-filled crawl on crutches. I found Yumoto Sensei and in my best Japanese I tried to explain the situation. I had looked up the word cartilage in my pocket dictionary and was disgusted to find that one of my favourite dishes at the local *izakaya*, a chewy fried dish that was called 'Chicken Nankotsu', was, in fact, fried chicken cartilage. Despite my nerves and the thought of all that cartilage I had eaten, I suppressed the urge to throw up, pointed at my balloon-sized knee and said '*nankotsu, nankotsu*' until Yumoto Sensei gave an understanding grunt. I then said – and to this day I don't know why – that it would take three weeks to heal. He seemed happy with this and I staggered away.

After about two weeks the swelling started to recede. I had already been doing physiotherapy to stop as much muscle wastage as possible, but after three weeks Aoife gave me an intensive programme to follow. Until my left leg was as strong as my right there would be no point going back as I was sure to re-injure myself and next time it would probably be worse. I went back to the *dojo* and said I would be another week. They weren't happy, but I thought the way I was still badly limping would have shown how injured I was. In hindsight I think they thought I was simply acting, which probably irritated them even more. After four weeks Aoife insisted I still wasn't ready. She was adamant I didn't go back and convinced me, over a rather delicious bottle of chardonnay, to do another week. Luckily Golden Week, a three-day holiday that is stretched to make a week (the Japanese make a habit of rather efficiently taking their time over things: holidays, work projects, war apologies) was the following week, so by saying to Yumoto Sensei that I would not be able to train until the following week

---

Izakaya. A Japanese bar/restaurant. The Japanese very rarely go to bars just to drink. Instead they prefer to disguise their binge-drinking by going to an izakaya and claim that their two small dishes of food between ten people constitutes eating out.

I gained two more weeks, bringing my total rehabilitation time to five weeks.

It was with particular trepidation that at the beginning of the second week of May I returned to the *dojo*. Over the last five weeks the attitude of Yumoto Sensei and my *sempai* had gone from moderately understanding to suspicious to just plain indifference as they ignored me even when I came to give news of my miraculous recovery. Afterwards I was relieved to find that my knee, despite taking a huge amount of punishment, had stood up to the test. I had also finished my first complete lesson of the instructors' course. I could die happy.

Whilst I was injured, life 'on' the instructors' course was great. I still went out drinking with the *hombu dojo* students – my friends – but now they called me *sensei*. John, a large Mexican who was my regular sparring partner, was constantly asking me what it was like to be in the inner circle and I was guilty of giving him some secret insights of the course despite having only trained with them once. There was always a certain amount of aloofness with the *hombu dojo sensei*. Students saw them as supermen and treated them with great reverence. This, I am sure, was in some ways promoted by the *sensei*, but, surprisingly it was also promoted by the students. They wanted someone to look up to, to follow in a small or maybe large way. So setting them apart allowed the *sensei* to fulfil a role that was prescribed by the students. John was excited that I was now taking on that role and becoming one of them. I tried to tell him that being injured meant I was being ignored, but he didn't listen. John was kind, very intelligent but lacked common sense. He spoke five languages, but none of them well. He was the type of person who would offer a lift to a jogger. He was a brilliant artist, poet and musician and had a burning desire to be invited on the instructors' course. But he was unable to see that as a huge, cumbersome thirty-eight-year-old, Yumoto Sensei believed he didn't have the youth or talent to fulfil his dream, but we were close and I think he was fulfilling his aspirations by proxy.

On my way to the *dojo* for a second day running it began to dawn on me that this was the beginning of a drawn-out ordeal. Although the class always started with an extensive warm-up, I quickly realized that all the *sensei* and *sempai* stretched a little before the lesson proper. I found a small, faraway corner and did the same. Yumoto Sensei came in.

'*Sueki, kumite,*' he grunted whilst nodding in my direction.

I jumped up, ready for nothing. We started sparring whilst everyone looked on. Sueki was tough. As vice-captain of the Teikyo University team he had spent four years on a karate scholarship. Teikyo was one of the 'karate universities'. Every year, Yumoto Sensei would travel to junior competitions looking for the toughest *karate-ka* of high-school leaving age. He would then offer a select few academic places at Teikyo and the chosen few would spend the next four years training diligently and winning competitions. Tournament success was their only goal and most team members ended up writing 'please excuse me, I am a member of the karate team' on their final academic exams. Sueki was no exception. He had graduated from Teikyo with a degree in law, but I am sure had only learnt what GBH meant. He was exceptional, however, in the sense that he had wanted to continue karate after graduation. On average Teikyo allows ten *karate-ka* per year to enter. For the eighteen-year-old kids it is a huge commitment as Teikyo training is infamous for its physically and mentally tough regime. To enter the university you have to live, breathe and sleep karate, you have to want it more than anything else in the world, although four years later about 90 per cent of graduates never do karate again.

Now I was facing one of the very few who continue training after they don't have to. He was lightning fast and his punches packed unbelievable power for a guy who was 5'7" and about ten kilos lighter than me. I was trying to pressurize him with a few attacks, but successful attempts were rare. The ultimate goal in *kumite* is to move without thought. Your mind should reach a Zen-like calm and attacks and blocks become entirely instinctive. When under pressure the calmness leaves you. The very time you need to be relaxed you tense up and throw telegraphed and weak attacks. Sueki predicted every attack like a weatherman predicts sun in the Sahara.

We had been sparring non-stop for about ten minutes, much longer than I was used to, when he slid in with a couple of punches aimed at my nose. I managed to block and duck out of the way, but as I was too tired and slow to move back we were face to face. To prevent any more attacks I grabbed hold of his arms. For the first time I felt a little stronger than him, and, unable to attack, he simply tried to struggle free. We had reached a stalemate. As I had a hold of him neither of us could do anything and I was about to let him go so we could start sparring again. As soon as my grip weakened he leapt up and head-butted me. Our heads clashed like two argumentative buffalo and I staggered back in disbelief – he had caught me on my mouth and my canine tooth had gone clear through my lower lip. Blood gushed out and my *dogi* quickly turned red.

'*Yame!*' Koyama Sempai dragged me into the toilet and gave me a tube of something that looked like Polyfilla. I was told to stuff it in the hole where my lip used to be and get back into the *dojo* pronto. I stood there looking at my face, my bloodstained *dogi* and this tube of Polyfilla. Trembling with fear and adrenaline, I realized I had little choice but to do as they wanted. Filling the hole in my lower lip wasn't the most pleasant experience of my life, but I felt nothing. I wiped the blood from my face, neck, chest and ear and returned to the *dojo*. The warm-ups had started and I quickly joined in. Apart from the gruesome ordeal of catching myself in the mirror and realizing, with my bloody *dogi* and swollen features, that I looked like a flesh-eating zombie, the rest of the lesson passed uneventfully. After we finished I got that increasingly familiar feeling of relief, although it was curtailed by Yumoto Sensei coming over to me.

'You should have been here everyday,' he said and walked away.

'Everyone was very unhappy with you.' Koyama Sempai had come over to interpret. He said that they had all been very angry with me because whilst I had been injured I should have continued to come to the *dojo* and watch the *kenshusei* training. This was the rule and I had broken it. I did consider pointing out to Koyama Sempai that he was the one who told me I didn't have to come to the *dojo* whilst I was doing physiotherapy, but, as I was quickly learning, the best reply to anything was 'yes, I understand. . .' Sometimes it is advisable to put a 'sorry' in there as well.

Sueki came up and asked if I was okay. It was the first act of kindness I had received whilst training with them. Slightly taken aback, I told him I was fine, it was nothing to worry about. I was the first ever *gaijin* he had spoken to and I think he was unsure of how to take me. However, I had given what he considered to be a very Japanese answer. It instantly relaxed him, so he went on to complain that I had very hard teeth. It was difficult to believe he hadn't knocked out my canine. He then pointed to his head where my tooth had left a small hole. He rubbed it and in a friendly, almost vulnerable voice, said it really hurt. I laughed and walked away. In some small way, it was the start of a great friendship.

* * *

As the *dojo* had only been open for a month or so, we were still putting the finishing touches to the place. Today's task was to put up the posters on the outside notice board. As if cries of fear and pain from the open windows weren't enough to advertise the place, it was decided that a picture of Yumoto Sensei, looking unfamiliarly friendly, would entice the local residents inside. Koyama Sempai and I went out to do the work. The bright May sunshine hurt my eyes. At the age of nine I had dropped a large bottle of Coke whilst trying to negotiate our garden gate, and because I had run home from the shops, the bottle was shaken and ready to burst. In those days the bottles were still glass and as it hit the ground I looked down and it exploded in my face. Glass shot everywhere, including a particularly determined piece that pierced my left cornea. Fortunately, due to the fantastic work of St Paul's Eye Hospital in Liverpool, a five-hour emergency operation saved my eye and I only lost 2 percent of my vision, although since then I had always found bright sunlight uncomfortable. I put my sunglasses on, only for Koyama Sempai to tell me to take them off immediately. I was quickly learning the rules. No sunglasses in front of one's seniors. I think it had something to do with direct eye contact, although I liked to believe that I just looked so much better than the rest of them in my Oakleys.

Struggling with the poster, I positioned it to the left then the right, a bit higher, no, a bit lower, until Koyama Sempai thought we had found the perfect position. We took a mind-bogglingly long time to do such a simple job, but it dawned on me that although Koyama Sempai had completed from the course, he was still very junior. He was hyper-aware of what his *sempai* thought of him and took great efforts to make sure he did the right thing. After years of abuse from his seniors he couldn't switch off from this constant vigilance, which seemed to be necessary for survival. (This was a distilled version of what I had seen in mainstream Japan: for example, staff at Navo would always overcomplicate tasks to show to the boss that they were doing a good job. I once had a lesson where by chance a boss and his subordinate attended. The subordinate normally had perfect English, but that couldn't be said for the boss, and I am positive the junior made deliberate mistakes to not make the boss look bad.) As I had been inching left and right with the poster a number of locals had gathered behind me, talking to Koyama Sempai. We were both in our *dogi* and they, from what I could pick up, were asking him about training times and prices. Eventually Koyama Sempai said perfection had been achieved and I turned around to meet our potential students. The look of horror on their faces is still with me. Surely most people who live in Tokyo are used to seeing *gaijin*? It wasn't until Koyama Sempai suggested I should go inside that it dawned on me that my bloodstained *dogi* and zombie features probably weren't the best advertisement for the *dojo*.

The course continued. Every morning I woke up feeling the same way. The pressure on Sueki and I was enormous and as time went by the cumulative effect was paralyzing. Sueki seemed to cope quite well. I never saw his blood, and he seemed to know all the secret rules. I, on the other hand, had to learn the hard way. I wished they would tell me what to do and what not to do. They were like old people who say to teenagers, 'Oh, if I only knew then what I know now...' and then don't go on to give you this vital knowledge. Takahashi Sempai was turning out to be my tormentor. He was constantly hovering, waiting for a mistake to be made. One of Sueki's and my tasks was to keep the *dojo* clean. Three or four times a week, after training, we would brush, mop and clean. We would get on our hands and knees and scrub the toilets and showers, vacuum the instructors' room and sort out the office. I felt like I was becoming the fittest, hardest housewife in Japan. We were like the highly trained cleaning branch of the SAS, but despite our diligence, mistakes were made, usually by me. One time, after I forgot to fill up the shampoo bottles, I received a bloodied nose. Another time for leaving the sweeping brush in the toilet, I acquired a black eye. I was constantly aware that every move I made was scrutinized and if I stepped one millimetre out of line I would be punished.

On one particular day, Takahashi Sempai had reached the end of his patience. He was usually in the office as I arrived to the *dojo*. With a bow, I had to say good morning in my politest Japanese. However, over the weeks the angle of my bow had been lacking and day by day I slowly infuriated him. On this day, what he considered to be his extensive patience had reached breaking point.

'Scott, *kumite*.' He called me over as soon as training finished. '*Osu sempai*.' I scurried over.

What followed was twenty minutes of horrific violence. He battered me from one end of the *dojo* to the other whilst the others watched passively. Exhausted by normal training, I wasn't able to put up much of a defence; in fact I had trouble standing. Despite having done the same training as me, Takahashi Sempai looked as if his turbo charge had just kicked in and he was revving up for the main event. It was pure stubbornness that made me get to my feet every time he dropped me.

Over the past couple of weeks I had learnt that getting hit didn't really hurt, apart from the small instant of pain on impact. Like children who fall over, then stand up and only after realizing what has happened start crying through shock, being beaten up is much the same. As long as I didn't allow the shock of being hit to get the better of me, then I would always be able to take the punishment. Every time I found myself facing the floor I knew that that particular attack was over, the pain was fleeting and all I had to do was stand up again and this particular session was bound to end soon. I remember being on the ground muttering to myself, 'Get up! Get up!' until I eventually stood.

Thankfully it did end and I was told to go into the toilet to clean myself up. I didn't need any human glue this time, so I wiped the blood away and looked at myself in the mirror. As I did, I had the strangest reaction. It was a reaction that I would become very familiar with over the next couple of months: I started to laugh. At first I didn't have a clue why, and I am sure people knowledgeable in this area would say I was in shock, but in time I came to think of it as a mixture of relief and pride. The relief part is obvious, but the pride was that I hadn't been beaten. Right from the beginning it had been made clear that they didn't want me on the course. They were trying to do everything to get me to quit, so every time they failed, it made me stronger and them weaker. Years later Takahashi Sempai would comment that he was amazed at how tough I was.

He never quite got over the fact that he could beat me as hard as he wanted, but like some human Weeble, I always came wobbling back for more. But at the time, I just looked at myself in the mirror and laughed. Koyama Sempai came in, pretending to go the toilet.

'Takahashi Sempai thinks your morning bow should be deeper.'

He was being very kind to me, so I refrained from asking whether he thought this information would have been of some use a couple of days ago.

'I will try harder to learn the rules,' I informed him.

The problem was I wasn't Japanese. I would never be able to intrinsically know what was the right and wrong thing to do and Takahashi Sempai took advantage of this.

Walking home, I tried to ignore the stares of the Japanese businessmen who had probably never seen a *gaijin* up close before, let alone one who looked like Freddy Kruger on a bad-hair day. At this time of year, just after the rainy season and before the suffocating humidity of high summer, the weather starts to warm up. I decided to walk to Ikebukuro. It was twenty-five minutes by foot so I normally took a train, where I would transfer to the Yurakacho subway line, which would take me back to my home station of Eidan Akatsuka. But on this particular afternoon I couldn't face the circular Yamanote line that took me from the *dojo* to Ikebukuro. I decided a stroll would be good for the soul.

As I approached Ikebukuro I passed a large police station. It was easy to spot. while criminals deliberated bank robberies and insane messiahs planned gas attacks on the subway, the elite police units stood outside the station checking *gaijin* cards and stopping innocent people on bikes to inspect their registration numbers. As a member of the elite *gaijin* -card-checking unit slimed up to me, I heard an almighty WHACK, followed by a scream. Looking up I could see it had come from the top window of the police station, but before I could turn around to see if any other innocent victim of the police's racial profiling had heard the same, another whack and scream came again; then another and another. They kept coming until the obvious torture and abuse that was taking place up there was undeniable. I had visions of a row of *gaijin* who had forgotten to re-register their cheap second-hand bikes or who had failed to turn up to the local district office to be fingerprinted when they first arrived, being lined up and beaten by rubber hosing or telephone directories. I looked around for the slightest of acknowledgements of what was going on. The police were oblivious to most things, including torture right under their noses, but even passers-by and fellow *gaijin* failed to see the significance of the events unfolding above us. I stood, as my *gaijin* card details were scrutinized, transfixed on the window, feeling powerless and strangely homesick. My card was shoved back at me without an acknowledgment of my legitimate right to be in the country and I started to walk away. The screams were still loud and the whacks seemed more ferocious. Just then, from one end of the long window, I saw a guy in a full protective outfit, holding his bamboo sword in his gloved hand: of course, *Kendo* – the Japanese art of swordsmanship. From inside I could still hear the whacks and the screams, but the whacks sounded similar to what I would imagine bamboo sounds like when hitting *kendo* protective gear and the shouts suddenly became identical to the "*kiai*" shouts that I made during training. As my indignation subsided I walked away, at a loss to make sense of events. The moment at the police station wasn't any great metaphor to how my life was progressing but it was typical of how badly I understood what was going on around me. I was lost, and every day I faced new challenges and puzzles. Moreover, I wasn't quite sure whether I had the right knowledge and equipment to deal with it all.

The days started to roll into one another. Time, when you are fixed into a solid and unchanging routine, has a habit of standing still, and the weeks passed by without my detection – that is not to say that they didn't pass by painfully, because they did. I was conscious of a change in the relationship between me and my fellow *karate-ka* at the *hombu dojo*. Before entering the course, I had many friends and we used to train and drink together. Drinking in Japan is a great hobby. The *izakaya* system is the perfect facilitator for a good time. Long tables and the politeness and efficiency of the ubiquitous staff further help you along your merry way. The karate crowd was made up of a good cross-section of Japanese society: rich businessmen, poor students, housewives and the occasional *gaijin*. Suzuki-san was a rather rotund senior black belt from the *dojo* and drinking with him was a treat. Upon arriving, he would pick up the menu, survey what was on offer and then ask for something completely different, but delicious. As was the social norm, he would order for everyone. Drinks arrived and the party would start. I was always a fan of grapefruit sour. You are given a large, litre-sized glass filled with ice, soda water and *shochu* – a clear spirit made from various unnamed grains. On the side would be a whole grapefruit that needed to be squeezed and poured into the glass. It was like drinking fruit juice and never gave me hangovers. Others would order racks of sake and a plank would arrive with small glasses of different type of rice wine. Some would order beer and small barrels would be brought to the table for people to help themselves to, and at the end of the evening Suzuki-san would disappear, returning with a receipt in his hand, which he would later put down to expenses and we would all leave thanking him for his generosity.

Once I entered the course, things changed irrevocably. Being part of the course meant a great deal to me, but what I didn't reckon on was how much it meant to others. A common interest – karate – had laid the foundation for what had become great friendships. However, as *kenshusei*, I was now *sensei* and this produced a new set of social rules. At first I resisted falling into the role that my friends were prescribing. I hated being called *sensei* outside the *dojo* and the constant 'topping up' of my beer glass only irritated me. I didn't see it as the height of respect, but my role as *sensei* was unchangeable and rigid and it didn't really matter what I wanted – what was more important were the wishes of the *hombu dojo* students. This social shift also represented the change in my training. Before, we had all shared common experiences through training. Particularly tough sessions were communally discussed over beer, but now the only time we talked about training was when they asked me technical questions. Before entering the course, we did normal karate. That type of training could be recognized in any *dojo*, in any country in the world. Now I had taken a new direction. The karate I was doing no longer resembled that of normal people and I think being calling *sensei* was a way of showing this. All I knew was that I wasn't doing anything that seemed like the karate I had loved for so long and I also had no idea where this new direction would take me.

Thankfully, it very quickly became clear that I had a friend on the course. Despite having to try to kill me when Yumoto Sensei gave him the nod, Sueki was becoming a close ally. Like the close bonds that are created in normal training, our friendship grew from the common ground that was the brutality of the course. I am sure his family and friends found it hard to relate to what he was going through, so I was the only person who could show real empathy. This closeness manifested itself in many ways: the slowing down of *kumite* drills when Yumoto Sensei wasn't looking, making fun of our *sempai* behind their backs, the odd pat of encouragement on the bum whilst training (a very Japanese thing, which I never quite understood nor became comfortable with). Remarkably, we never openly discussed the hardships. It was almost like one of the unwritten rules with which I was constantly battling and I wasn't quite sure if Sueki would try to beat me up if I broke it.

As the summer started to turn up the temperature and the humidity reached steam-room thickness, I reluctantly settled into the course. Despite Sueki's friendship, looking back it is easy to see how desperately unhappy I was. It wasn't that I had learnt to handle the training and uncertainty that I faced every day, it was more that I had just become numb to it. My emotions had taken such a battering over the first couple of months that they no longer felt anything. I found that from 2 pm on Friday afternoon until bedtime Sunday evenings I was allowed to live. As I walked out of the *dojo* on Fridays my emotions came out for a breather and refreshing walk. However, as I fell asleep Sunday night I knew I would be opening my eyes to life as a *kenshusei* and my emotions would close down again. My weekends slowly turned into binge-drinking excursions around Tokyo, although I had a rule not to drink during the week, as I couldn't face training with a hangover.

As weekdays involved further excursions into the realms of depression, despair and madness, I found sleeping to be the best form of escape. I slept as late as possible until I had to get up to go to the *dojo*. I would return home at about 2.30 pm, eat lunch quickly and sleep again before my first student arrived at 3 pm. No matter how short the time was, I could suddenly sleep at the drop of a hat. Usually I would teach until 5 pm, at which point I would pull out my futon and again sleep until 7 pm when my evening students arrived. Finishing work at 9 pm I would have some dinner, watch a little television and then be asleep by 11.30 pm, not waking the following morning until 10.30 am. I was sleeping up to fourteen or fifteen hours a day, anything to escape the horror. Little did I know I was going mad.

My apartment of 4 years –
futon put away, this was the daytime look.

Eiden Akatsuka –
the small village within Tokyo that I called home.

The Instructors' name board at the JKS Hombu Dojo – my name
is bottom left under "Hombu Dojo Instructors based abroad".

Competing in the 1999 European Championships in Ireland –
I won gold and bronze.

The entrance to the JKS Hombu Dojo.

Teaching at the Hombu Dojo, my only pleasure.
The classes did get bigger.

合格通知

スコット　ラングレー
S c o t t　L a n g l e y

貴殿、審査の結果、本会の修行生として合格したことを通知する。

平成１２年４月２日

武道社団　日本空手松涛会

首席師範　浅井　哲彦

My official invite to enter the JKS Instructors' Course –
Shugyosei.

Taken at the start of the course, I still looked somewhat
fresh-faced and happy.

Group photo taken in January 2001 at the JKS Hombu Dojo.
I look happy, but the empty beer glass (bottom right) explains
why.

Taken towards the end of the first year,
the stress is starting to take its toll.

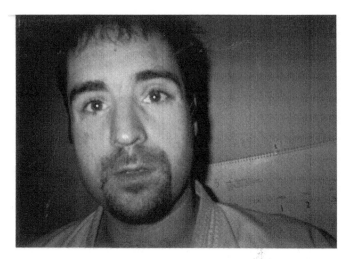

Taken in the summer of the second year.

Group photo of Kangeiko 2002. The dojo had grown bigger and
I look happy before I had started drinking.

Chapter Five:

OCD

I open my right eye – it has to be my right eye – and look at the digital clock on my VCR. It says 10.34 am. I still have three minutes left and so I go back to sleep. I know I have slept as I have had the same dream, the one which involves me standing in the middle of the *dojo*, panic stricken. I open my right eye again and sure enough it is 10.37 am. I jump up as there is not a moment to lose. Quickly the futon is folded and thrown into the closet. Next I have to get to the toilet. I arrive to find the far cubicle is being used. Despite there being two other vacant loos available, I wait. It has to be the far one. Eventually the phantom shagger, who lives above me, emerges from the toilet and I dash in. I am already behind schedule.

After my business is done – it has to be number two, no matter what – I quickly go to the shower room. The shower must go on first and, whilst trying to avoid the spray, I get undressed. I wash my hair, then body and finally I have a shave. Shaving in my room, with a mirror, would be so much easier, but that isn't the way it must be done. I arrive back to my room and check the clock. It is 10.50 am, dead on time. I dress, check my phone for messages, pack my bag and then sit on my small coffee table and look at the clock again. It is now 10.54 am, and there are three minutes to wait. I am trying not to think of what I will face in my near and inescapable future, but before I know it, it is 10.57 am. I must leave now.

I cycle to the station, having taken my familiar route, and park my bike in my beloved place. Fortunately the little gap between the phone box and the railing is free, sometimes it isn't and I have to move a stranger's bike from my place to the other side of the phone box, where there is always ample room. I have often been given funny looks by passers-by, but this time I am spared the inquisition. I dash into the station and look at the clock. Perfect timing, 11 am. As I walk down the stairs to the platform, I can feel the wind being forced towards me as the train arrives. I walk along the platform as the carriages are pulling up, and just before the doors open, I sit down on the middle chair of the middle row of seats, situated in the middle of the platform. I watch people get on and off, the doors close and I watch the train leave at exactly 11.02 am. I wait for a further five minutes until the 11.07 am arrives and I get on. Guaranteed of being able to sit on my seat, this train only starts one station up. The carriage is virtually deserted so I sit down and fall into my fear-induced sleep. Two stops down I wake up to see the old lady with shopping get on and sit opposite me, like she does most days. I then fall asleep again.

At 11.19 am the train pulls into Ikebukuro station, I stagger out, run up the escalator, through the ticket barrier and onto the *Yamanote* line. Arriving just as the 11.21 am train pulls in, I let all the *sararimen* get on and then wait, ensuring I will be at the front of the queue for the next train. The 11.26 am arrives and I dart on to get my seat again. There are plenty available, but my seat, the one next to the door, is always popular as you can lean your head against the rail and sleep. Again this time I am lucky, as I shoulder-barge some anonymous suit out of the way, and sit down. One stop down and again I pull myself out of my panic-stricken sleep to see the smelly guy with the baseball cap get on. He is here to collect *Manga* – often sexually explicit adult comics -

76

that have been discarded by this morning's commuters and he will re-sell them to the same commuters this evening.

The train arrives at *Sugamo*, I get off, make my way to the stairs, avoid the escalators, walk out the ticket gates and check the time. It says 11.31 am. Perfect timing again. I head to the dojo, take a deep breath and open the door. The rest is up to them. I have gone beyond hell. I have found myself in the world of obsessive compulsive disorder.

By the summer of 2000, the stress of the course had started to manifest itself into what could romantically be described as idiosyncratic behaviour. Of course I am self-diagnosing when I say I had obsessive compulsive disorder, but I am sure few would disagree with saying something was seriously wrong. I had, in a few short months, created a comprehensive ritual, which began the moment I woke up – in fact, dictated the moment I woke up – and finished the moment I stepped foot into the *dojo*.

I was obsessed with time and the meaning of each number on the digital clocks. When checking the schedule, I never used my own watch as it wasn't digital, and the numbers couldn't be added up. Fortunately, I lived in a digital city and was surrounded by LCD clocks. I got up at 10.37 am because $1+0+3+7=11$ and then $1+1=2$, which represented Sueki and I. Maybe if I got up at that time there would only be Sueki and I at the *dojo* – a possibility, albeit highly unlikely. I left home at 10.57 am because the numbers added up to 4 which represented the four main people who were always training, Yumoto, Takahashi, Sueki and me. I arrived at 11 am because this equalled 2: Sueki and I. And I got onto the 11.07 am train because the 11 represented Sueki and me and number 7 was lucky. Arriving in Ikebukuro at 11.19 am was out of my control, but getting the 11.26 am was good as it added up to 1 and that meant just me, alone in the *dojo*! Finally, getting into Sugamo at 11.31 am was something of a challenge. The clock was always just about to change so I had to rush out the door and up the station to where the digital clock hung (the escalators would have been quicker, but for some reason that escapes me now, I barred this option from my manic world). The times of 11.31 am or 11.32 am were both good. The first represented me alone and the second represented Sueki and I. Occasionally I would arrive at 11.33 am and this, in my mind, spelled disaster. The point is I was constantly aware of what time it was and what mystical implications it would have on the day's training.

Other parts of the ritual involved doing things in a specific order: waking up, going to the toilet, washing, changing and finally leaving the house in precisely the same manner. I often consoled myself by thinking that many people have routines. Routine is the foundation of most people's daily life, but this went way beyond simple habits and I came to believe that by following this routine, the instructors' course training would somehow be made easier. In truth, my logic was sound. On previous days I had followed this process and the day concluded in me surviving the training. Therefore it was natural to think that there was a direct correlation between the process of getting myself to the *dojo* and then surviving what went on during training. My vulnerable frame of mind needed all the reassurance it could get. However, it is difficult to remember how it all came about, and I only recall a fully formed pattern. I cannot remember the crucial moment that crossed me over to this way of thinking, but from very early on, life on the instructors' course was dictated by a severe and inflexible following of the code.

I also built into this routine little ways of boosting my confidence, especially on days when I knew I had screwed up at the *dojo* and knew I would be punished. The old lady with the shopping bizarrely represented Yumoto Sensei and if I managed to see her on the way to Ikebukuro, then that meant that Yumoto Sensei would not be at training. I didn't have visions of him doing the weekly shop at the local supermarket, but I felt the odds of him not being at the *dojo* greatly increased with her appearance. The smelly guy with the baseball cap was Takahashi Sempai and again seeing the *manga* collector promoted the chances that Takahashi

Sempai would not be at training. The whole ceremony of getting to the *dojo* was a way of giving me enough confidence to open the door and walk in.

By July, the heat and humidity were unbearable. Energy was sapped away by even simple things like cycling to the station. All *kenshusei* were expected to take part in the morning class, starting at 10.30 am. However, doing an extra hour before training started proper was what could politely be termed troublesome. Still teaching English part time, I invented students who wanted lessons in the mornings. Not wanting me to end up destitute and find himself financially responsible, Yumoto Sensei agreed that I would be allowed to teach before class and come to the *dojo* for instructors' training only, which started at 12 pm.

I would arrive to the chill of an air-conditioned *dojo* just as the morning class was finishing. It was then turned off the instant I got changed and the windows were flung open. During the summer months the temperature can reach 38°C, and this, coupled with killer humidity, made for horrific lessons. As usual, we would start off by facing the mirror and do hundreds of punches and kicks. After about thirty minutes of this and before the inevitable *kumite* would finish both me and the lesson off, we always moved to the back of the *dojo* and practise *ido kihon*. I was learning that this was the best time: being close to the window, there would always be a small draft that I would pretend was cooling me off between sets of twenty techniques. Also, the window faced the garden, which was typically Japanese, with a small waterfall, stream and a pond at one end with koi carp in it. Whilst getting my breath back I would, in a bid to cool down – although it seems somewhat absurd now – pretend I was one of the koi, swimming in the water. Often, whilst relentlessly charging up and down the *dojo*, all I could think about was getting back to the window and watching the fish swim. But Tokyo is festooned with crows. The metropolis can be considered a clean city, but huge bins and refuge dumps are hidden down every alley and behind every building. The Japanese national pastime is eating and shopping and overpacking of the over-consumed goods helps to produce fifty million tonnes of waste per year. As a result, crows have grown to gargantuan sizes, feeding off these spoils. Over the summer months, the massive birds had sourced fresher food and taken it upon themselves to eat the fish. One by one the beautiful golden koi disappeared from the pond, and as it got hotter, my ability to project myself into the pond, via the fish, diminished. By mid July there was only one left. I expected to turn up someday soon to find that not only the last fish, but also my ability to resist this heat, had gone.

The days passed, then the weeks, and still by mid August the fish remained elusive. One day, in a moment of unexpected friend-liness, Yumoto Sensei told me that this koi must be very intelligent as every time a crow came near the garden it would hide under an overhanging rock. Slowly, somewhere deep in my psyche I started to identify with this magical koi. Again, looking back, I can't quite remember what brought on this bizarre behaviour. I was probably too busy trying to stay alive to speculate on the reasons for my behavioural changes. However, no matter how subtle the changes were, they did take effect, and before I knew it, my only pleasure during training was watching the fish swim in the cool water and empathising with its fight against the evil crows. I only wished that, I too, had somewhere to hide.

I once watched a documentary on the selection process of the SAS (I had been fascinated with the regiment since childhood). In this particular programme, a candidate spoke about how he was taking one day at a time; in fact, one hour at a time. He felt that if he looked forward any further than the next couple of hours, the horror of what he was facing would break him and he would quickly give up. I was doing the same. I no longer thought about anything other than getting myself to the *dojo* in the mornings, and from that moment on I felt and thought absolutely nothing. Apart from a few vague images and the obvious emotional memory of fear and pain, I don't remember anything concrete, and can only piece together vague memories of what I presume happened.

I thought it couldn't get any worse, but at the beginning of August, Koyama Sempai left. He had graduated from the course in March, then had spent the spring and summer organizing what he wanted to do. His girlfriend was French and through her contacts he had been offered a teaching post with a large karate association in France. It was his dream job and he left as soon as he could. I had known him and his girlfriend from the first day I arrived at the *hombu dojo* and they had become great friends. When Jen left me and I was abandoned in Japan, Koyama Sempai was one of the few Japanese people who took time to see if I was OK. When I had trouble with my knee and couldn't make it to the *dojo*, we still met, drank and he kept me informed about what was happening there. And even though he still scared me witless, had stamped on my head, told me vital rules and information after I had got a beating, he had shown me compassion and never once became irritated by my insufficient grasp of the situation. Never fazed by the constant need for him to translate, even during the toughest of training sessions, I was so sad to see him go. On his final day I helped him pack his things. We always spoke in English, as my Japanese still wasn't up to scratch, plus no one else knew what we were talking about. As I folded his blood-stained sparring mitts and sweat towel away in a box he quietly started to talk.

'I am so happy to leave,' he said, to my amazement.

'Really?' I wanted to ask why. He was as strong as a bull and had the physique to match, like a cross between Hulk Hogan and Bruce Lee. Combining his strength with astounding speed, he was one of the best fighters I had sadly paired up with in Japan. Amazingly – although in hindsight, I don't know why I was so surprised – he had counted down the days to graduation and during the course he had come to hate karate. He was desperate to leave. I was desperate for him to stay.

It dawned on me that I was now the only one who could speak

English in the *dojo*. Until Koyama Sempai left for good, I was too numb to realize that most things that were said to me were translated through him. I could get general directions and instructions on what we should be doing, but specific insults often went over my head. On the first day after Koyama Sempai left I realized how much I had relied on him. Takahashi Sempai spat something out and I just stood there, like a rabbit looking straight at an oncoming car. He spat it out again.

'I am sorry *sempai*. I do not understand.' I grovelled a very polite reply in Japanese. He stormed off whilst grinding one fist into his other hand. Later he would grind the same fist into my face.

By mid August it had become obvious that Takahashi Sempai had been given the job of bringing me up to standard. I saw him as my nemesis. He educated me by the constant application of threats followed by fulfilment of those threats, and reduced me to a nervous wreck. By the second week of August the immense pressure of the course seemed directly proportional to the heat and humidity of the Tokyo summer. One of the hottest in living memory, I remember an old woman had died from heat exhaustion not so far from the *dojo*. However, the windows still stayed open and the air conditioner still stayed off. Towards the end of one of the sessions we finished off with the normal *jiyu-kumite*. Inevitably for the last fight I ended up with Takahashi Sempai. After a few near–misses and some non-misses, which weren't strong enough to knock me out, he landed an almighty punch to the mouth. Blood instantly splattered the walls and floor – he had put the familiar canine tooth through the bottom of my mouth. As I unhooked the flapping wound, I saw Takahashi Sempai rub his knuckle. He had hit me so hard, the canine had also left a hole in his index-finger knuckle. To stop my mouth from turning the *dojo* floor crimson, I excused myself and ran to the toilet for more of my favourite Polyfilla. On my return, Takahashi Sempai was still nursing his hand and looked none too pleased.

'Scott, do you brush your teeth every morning before you come to the *dojo*?'

'Yes, *sempai*.' I didn't know where this was leading, but I felt compliance was the best strategy.

'Good, well make sure you do, as I don't want to get an infection in my hand.'

I promised I would but as I showered and left, and as my mind and my emotions reawakened for the remainder of the day, I started to think: what sort of world am I living in where it is my responsibility to stop my *sempai* from getting an infections when he tries to knock my teeth out? Answer: the world of the instructors' course.

Several weeks later my mouth had just about healed up, but I noticed that Takahashi Sempai's hand was still quite bad. 'Yes,' I thought, 'my body heals faster. I am the strongest!' It was all I needed to push myself on a little further.

That weekend I had to get away. Anne 'the physio' had asked me to escape with her to a coastal resort about two hours from Tokyo. There would be others, but with the noticeable exception of her boyfriend. I jumped at the chance. Friday evening we travelled by the famous bullet train *shinkansen* down to Shizuoka, a coastal resort two hours from Tokyo, and stayed at a family run *ryokan*. With the pretence of saving money we shared a room and I finally had something to take my mind off the past couple of weeks.

Japanese seaside resorts are similar to many you would find in the Mediterranean area. What were once sleepy fishing villages are now commercialized towns that spring to life at the beginning of summer and then hibernate again as autumn approaches. However, there is always a Japanese twist. Ice-cream parlours are replaced by vendors selling shaved ice with delicious fruit syrups squirted on top. Fish and chips are replaced with local, daily caught fish, served raw. And instead of concrete monstrosities blighting the once-perfect vista, old bamboo and rice-paper-constructed pensions litter the coastline. Without the chaos of city living, the people are more relaxed, friendly and life seems to slow down. It had been such a long time since I had been away. Whilst at university I had very little money – and admittedly no need – to go on holiday, and since coming to Japan, every holiday I returned to the UK to see my family. So no matter how short it was, I was going to make the best out of my little trip... and maybe even begin a little holiday romance.

The *ryokan* was basic, but just around the corner was a great bar and restaurant populated by what seemed to be the entire expat workforce of PricewaterhouseCoopers: rich, arrogant Americans, English and Australians who had second homes in the area. I didn't quite fit in.

'Sebastian, this is my very good friend, Scott.' Anne, with her arm linking mine, introduced me to a few friends.

'*Hajimemashite.*' Sebastian obviously spoke Japanese.

'*Yoroshiku Onegashimasu.*' My Japanese was better.

'So, Scott, what do you do?' This is where the conversation was about to end.

'I am a student.' My standard answer. Whether I was speaking Japanese or not, most people would presume I studied the language and leave it at that. The more genuinely interested people would ask where was I studying, or on the very rare occasion, what was I studying. I often took this as a bona fide curiosity to know what I was doing, so I would give them a romanticized version of what I did, which most of them still found gruesome. However, on this occasion I never got past the presumption of a language student.

'Oh.' Sebastian walked away. As too did everyone else that night. Students, in their world, had nothing to offer them as a friend/acquaintance. I drank a large amount of wine and returned to the *ryokan* once Anne had finished talking to each patron of the bar about her problems with her boyfriend. At least, I thought, this night wasn't going to be a complete waste.

'Scott, you're great, thanks for being such a good mate. Night.'

Stunned, and alone, I crawled to my futon.

The Saturday went no better. More friends – friends of her

boyfriend – arrived, and the little time we had had alone was over. I sat on the beach and combined sunbathing with sulking, knowing holiday romance was not going to happen now. At the very least I would go home with a tan. I read my book, drank a beer and dozed off. I awoke in agony. I had fallen asleep with my Oakleys on and paid the price. The shades had protected my eyes completely from the sun, so when I removed the glasses I looked like a panda bear that had been skinned and boiled alive and then released back into the wild. That evening, like an escaped burns victim, I hobbled to the bar. The worst of the scorching was around my ankles and every time I moved, my shoes dug into enflamed areas. I shuffled to a quiet corner, only to watch Anne do the rounds again, whilst I tried to induce numbness through alcohol. The evening was a painful and lonely way to escape Tokyo and from that moment on I knew that my time here would be a disappointingly complete and dismal failure. I returned home Sunday evening frustrated and in pain, only for the stress of the instructors' course to return in full.

The next morning I tottered to the *dojo*, still in pain. I had to bandage my ankles as they had started to blister, but Takahashi Sempai was not pleased with the way I looked. Obviously I had been in the sun, and I didn't know what angered him more, my appearance or the fact that I had had a weekend away. During the final *kumite* stage of the lesson, he battered me severely. Vindictively, he kept trying to *ashi-bari* my legs, but instead of sweeping from the side, which drops you quicker than a granny on winter ice, his foot blows came from the front, straight onto my blisters. The result was that my left eye was now black, my right was still very white, both legs had been skinned and the oozing liquid from the blisters was now turning red with blood. After training he took me aside.

'You are *kenshusei*.' He spoke in very clear Japanese. 'You are JKS *kenshusei*.'

85

'*Osu.*' Technically I was *shugyosei*, but I wasn't about to argue the point.

'You always represent the JKS. Every minute. Every day. The way you look is shameful!'

The following weekend was the All-Japan Championships, which this year were being held in Kyushu, the southernmost island of mainland Japan. Plane tickets had been booked, hotels reserved and schedules made. Remarkably, I had been included in them. I was about to get my first freebie from the JKS, although I was paying for it in other ways. Apparently, the *hombu dojo* was asked to give a demonstration at the championships. Yumoto Sensei, with Takahashi Sempai, Sueki and me, put together a piece that would delight the crowd.

I had done this type of thing before, but I had never been the attacker. With demonstrations there is always the innocent victim (Yumoto Sensei, how ironic) and the thug-like evil attackers: Takahashi fitted the bill, but Sueki and I were unfairly cast. The idea was for the three of us to spontaneously attack Yumoto Sensei, and he, with Jason Bourne finesse, would defend the honour of the JKS. That was the idea, and I am sure that is what it looked like to the audience, but in reality it was three hard weeks of thirty minutes' drilling after each training session. Yumoto Sensei also easily blocked the predetermined attack, delivering bone-crunching counters that needed very little acting to show the devastation that he *could* have caused. I wondered what it was going to be like on the day, if he hit so hard in practice.

True to form, I arrived at the airport late and angered everyone there, including Taguchi Sensei, ninth dan, our chief instructor. At sixty-seven years old, 5'2' and about eight stone, he was a slight and weak-looking man. However, I had trained many times with him in the UK and had learnt never to underestimate him. I think I had seen him only once since I took the test for the course, but I knew he was kept up to date with our progress. He obviously knew the difficulties Yumoto Sensei and Takahashi Sempai were having with me and his look and demeanour said it all. I apologized and tried to explain that until one frantic hour ago I had not known that there were two airports in Tokyo, one for international (Narita) and the other for national flights (Haneda). With the help of a sergeant-major-like help-desk woman and the price of an astronomically expensive taxi, I had dashed across Tokyo and arrived on time. As I was doing so, they all just walked off. Only Sueki showed the slightest hint of interest, but at least I had got my point across.

* * *

Kyushu was green, natural and fresh – everything Tokyo was not. People looked darker, smaller and more rounded. They were charming and friendly in a way that didn't really exist in Tokyo. We were met by the chief instructor for the area, Maizu Sensei, and taken straight to his restaurant. It was covered wall to wall with medals, trophies and memorabilia of his competition days. I knew him from the early nineties when he used to come to teach in Europe. A warm, friendly guy, he was a seventh dan who had never done the instructors' course and therefore lacked that position and standing that went with graduation from the course. He also lacked that aloofness that *hombu dojo sensei* sometimes had. Well-respected and skilled, it was a refreshing change to be around someone who was the same rank as Yumoto Sensei, but didn't have the same intimidating and menacing stare. I had been with the group for six hours and the intensity of constant vigilance was exhausting. Sueki hadn't been too happy that we were all going to the competition and I quickly understood why. In the restaurant we were, as two lowly third dan, both constantly at the beck and call of all the *sempai* and *sensei*. In the hour or two that we had been there, more senior grades from around the country had arrived. The four dignitaries who had been at my test were there and we were surrounded by six or seven seventh, eighth and ninth dans. Meanwhile Takahashi Sempai and Yamada Sempai tried to get us drunk. Between filling glasses of beer or bringing food to the tables of the *sensei*, our glasses were being constantly topped up by our *sempai*. By 11 pm I was drunk. The continuous need to focus all my attention on the *sensei*, whilst trying to keep up the drinking games of our *sempai* was so draining that by the time I made it back to the hotel I was desperate to sleep and delighted to find that we were no longer needed to serve the *sensei* or amuse the *sempai*. Sueki and I, weary and drunk, escaped to our beds.

The next two days were not so bad. The competition area was immense. Before this, the largest tournament I had been part of had had about six areas that were constantly in use for the entire day; this had sixteen areas that were constantly in use for the entire two days. I was used to competing in the UK, where 80 per cent of the competitors were, at best, of a mediocre standard, where there were usually only two referees and a timekeeper per area and where most events, supposed to start at 10 am, started at 11 am and were finished by 5 pm with an hour for lunch. This was different: the standard was excellent and no one was below black belt. Each area had a team of eight referees and four officials. The event started at exactly 9 am and ran until 1 pm. We then had a thirty-minute break, when every competitor, team official and tournament official was given a complimentary *bento* – the exquisitely prepared lunch-boxes. It then started again at 1.30 pm and ran until 6 pm. Each category was given a time allocation and an area number, and give or take five or ten minutes, it ran perfectly. The second day everything ran until 2 pm when we broke for lunch. During lunch all the areas were moved and one large mat was set up in the middle of the hall for the finals. At 3 pm all the competitors filed in, led by the Kyushu marching band. After an opening speech by Taguchi Sensei, listened to by the thousand or so participants and thousands more spectators, the children's finals started. After that, there was the demonstration by the *hombu dojo*, followed by the adult finals. The whole event culminated in another speech by the chairman of the JKS and virtually dead on 7 pm the competition finished. Everyone went off to various bars and restaurants, where tables had been booked for 7.30 pm, and enjoyed the evening in what I presume was in equally scheduled fashion.

My success at the competition was somewhat varied. The demonstration was a huge success, albeit a nerve-wrecking experience. Walking out in front of thousands of people was made worse by my heavily bandaged and skinned shins in *Fame* -style leg warmers. Compounded by the fact that I was about to act like I was trying to kill Yumoto Sensei, my anxiety was reaching record levels. What happened was the complete opposite from what we were trying to portray. As I had suspected, Yumoto Sensei battered us. In what was a terrifying – but what the audience thought was an awesome – display of power, speed and timing, Takahashi Sempai, Sueki and I were thrown, punched and kicked about the area as if we were made of rice paper. As the demonstration reached its climactic end, the crowd literally went wild, stomping on the benches, wolf-whistling and waving their individual *dojo* flags. By Japanese standards it was quite rock and roll. Yumoto Sensei was satisfied (happy would be overstating his mood) and, therefore, so was I, despite the foot-shaped bruise slowly blooming across my chest.

The competition was a different matter. I did well in *kata*, getting through to the final sixteen, before losing against one of the *kata* specialist from Teikyo University. Some *karate-ka* specialise in only *kata* or *kumite*. They do this solely to win competitions, but it is not true karate. It is similar to American football, where they have separate offensive and defensive squads and therefore are crap at playing rugby.

In *kumite* I was less successful. I was relaxed as I thought whoever I faced in the competition would be far easier than facing Takahashi Sempai in the *dojo*. In the first round I was up against a guy from some backwater in Hokkaido, an easy opponent, but I froze – due, in hindsight, to a combination of stress and pressure to perform combined with the trauma of the past six months. The result was that I lost, not pathetically, but nonetheless I lost. Takahashi Sempai was furious.

'You will never lose against a normal *karate-ka* again.' I am not too sure if it was a prophecy or a command, but the beating I got the week after made me think it was the latter.

The Sunday night, after all the stress of competing and the demonstration, I was exhausted. (One thing the instructors' course taught you was the appreciation of the smaller things in life. I took great pleasure in the basics, such as access to water, being asleep and owning all my own teeth.) On this particular night I was only concentrating on getting to my hotel room and collapsing into bed. The night dragged on as the *sempai* became increasingly drunk. When talking with individuals I could understand the thrust of the conversation, but within a group of fast-talking, drunk karate *sensei* and *sempai*, I was lost, so I kept my mouth shut and head down and as the hours went by I switched off. It was a vital mistake.

Sitting next to Shima Sempai, I was into a false sense of security. He didn't often train on the course and when he did, he was never particularly bloodthirsty. Kind and considerate, even to me, he always had a bit of advice and was quite supportive. However, as the night wore on, he got increasingly drunk, until eventually, speaking with his hands, he managed to spill his wine. Meanwhile, I, in a stress-induced coma, took a second longer than I should have to react to the incident. Being sat next to him, I should have been the first to react and deal with the spillage but instead it was Takahashi Sempai, a junior of Shima Sempai, who jumped to attention. Both Takahashi Sempai and Yamada Sempai were furious and within what seemed like seconds it was decided that I had to attend the Teikyo *Gasshuku* to learn manners. A *gasshuku* is a residential training camp, where people come together to forge good spirits. In the west these tend to be weekend affairs where you train maybe ten hours over the three days and build up a sense of camaraderie in the bar. Held at various venues all over Japan, I quickly became aware that the Teikyo *Gasshuku* was something completely different. It lasts seven days, with seven hours of training a day. I was told that Carlos Martin had refused to do the course and Richard Amos had only managed three days before he fled to the relative safety of Tokyo (I later found out that these two facts weren't entirely true – history, it seems, is written by the victors). I was then told that if I did not complete the whole *gasshuku* I would be thrown off the instructors' course.

I returned to Tokyo the following day. As we had been busy all weekend, we had the Monday off, but when I turned up for training on the Tuesday, I found, to my horror, that some fast-diving crow had taken my magical koi. As I suspected, with that fish, my last remaining ounce of determination and resolve had gone. As August drew to an end the humidity and heat that I had battled against all summer was finally easing, but with the prospect of the *gasshuku* in the first week of September looming, I felt no benefit. Tired and lonely, I waited it out, knowing that they had finally broken me and that this may be the end.

Chapter Six:

If You Can't Take a Joke...

I am being kicked awake by an eighteen-year-old whose seniority means that I have to comply immediately. Jumping into my *dogi*, I tiptoe to the allocated rooms and gently lull the Second Years out of subconsciousness. I then retreat to my room and, in silence, put away my *futon*, tidy the limited space that is designated as mine and then, with the rest of the First Years, hurry outside a good ten minutes before anyone else. We wait in an uneasy silence.

The Second and Third Years join us and once the remaining lazy Fourth Years emerge from the *ryokan*, we set off on a gentle jog. Past deserted post offices, schools, shops and the train station, I am trying to put out of my mind the day's schedule. I know the first Tokyo-bound train leaves in less than forty-five minutes. It would be so easy to pack up and get on it. I could be home in two hours.

Back at the *ryokan* the mad rush starts again. Off with the *dogi*, on with the tracksuit, we First Years hustle into the kitchen and begin preparing breakfast. The fish is already cooked for us by the kitchen staff but our instructions are to prepare the rice, miso soup, tea and bread. We do it quickly before the Second, Third and Fourth Years file in. Sitting quietly on our allocated chairs, we wait... and wait. After about fifteen minutes, Yumoto Sensei arrives. Jumping up and deeply bowing at the same time (not easy) we all say good morning. He grunts and sits down and we all follow suit. He starts to eat and so do we. People begin to relax and the Fourth Years talk to Yumoto Sensei and all the O-B – Old-Boy, the alumni of the university. The Third Years talk amongst themselves, the Second Years whisper quietly and we First Years try not to breathe.

After breakfast has been eaten the First Years clear up. Masaki and I rush to the dojo and prepare the cold tea and clean towels. Grabbing a brush each, we sweep up all the bugs and creepy-crawlies that have gathered in the night. Just as we are finishing the rest of the First Years arrive, followed by the Second, Third and finally the Fourth years. Making a circle the warm-ups start. Training begins. With gut-wrenching anxiety, I stretch, twist and sweat, waiting for Yumoto Sensei to arrive. Perfectly timed, he arrives just as the warm-ups end, and the three-hour session starts.

With a split lip and bleeding nose, I make my way back to the *ryokan* to help prepare lunch. Again we ritualistically wait for Yumoto Sensei and then the First Years eat in silence whilst everyone talks about how hard they had hit one of us in the morning session. After lunch is cleared away, I escape to the room and manage to sleep for an hour until I am dragged awake. We return to the *dojo*. The same warm-up followed by a similar three-hour session ensues and I wearily make my way back to the *ryokan* for the third time that day.

Evening duties. First, all the *dogi* of our seniors must be washed. Then dinner is prepared and eaten. After dinner, the First Years set about the mammoth task of cleaning the dojo equipment and finally about thirty minutes before lights out we are finished. I nip to the local convenience store and ram chocolate down me like a man possessed and then stagger back to bed. I don't know where I am or what I am doing and I am too tired to care. Welcome to the Teikyo University Gasshuku.

'If you can't take a joke, you shouldn't have joined up!' I think he was a sergeant-major in the para regiment, giving an interview about the Falklands War and about how a number of his colleagues had been killed and injured during a particularly ferocious battle. After describing the brutality of war and the losses received by both sides, he kind of slipped the comment in as an afterthought. Since then I have heard many servicemen on many occasions using it to describe many wars. I guess it is just a way of numbing reality with humour to take the edge off the whole experience. It stuck in my mind as I was making my way to Tachikawa station, the designated rendezvous for the students of Teikyo University.

Having learnt my lesson the previous month from the 'meeting at the airport' fiasco, I didn't want to be late, so arrived thirty minutes ahead of schedule. Already members of the group were beginning to gather at the assembly point, but rather than join my future fellow torture victims, I decided to find a dimly lit corner of the vast station and wait the half hour. A week with these guys was enough; I didn't want to prolong the whole affair. Finding a bench, I shucked off my rucksack and sat on the seat. The all-too familiar feeling of panic-induced tiredness crept up and before I knew it, I was asleep in a position that coma victims would find hard to get comfy in. I must have looked like a homeless *gaijin*, as rare as an albino tiger. The dream of me standing in the *dojo*, drenched with sweat and fear, normally found its way into these little cat naps, and this time was no exception. When under extreme pressure I would dream that I was being hit and thrown about. With a jump, as Takahashi Sempai was landing a killer punch to the chin, I bounced awake. Checking my watch, I had five minutes to meeting time, so wanting to show my keenness, I gathered my things and returned to the meeting point. As I rounded the corner they were all there. Despite being early, I was the last to arrive.

'Morning, Scott-san.' Nakata, the captain, a battle-hardened and scarred twenty-two-year-old, greeted me pleasantly and handed me my train ticket.

'Thank you. Good morning.' I offered a friendly hello to the rest of the crowd. They looked on as if I was some puzzling toy they had been given to play with.

I followed the others along the track to the train, boarded, and, like clockwork, the train rolled out of the station. I wasn't too sure where we were going and as the ticket was all in *kanji*, it wasn't much of a clue. Apart from the captain, no one had said a word to me, but far from feeling an outcast, I was quite comfortable with the situation. If I was allowed to keep myself to myself in the moments when we were not training, then I was sure I would be able to get through this. Just like during the instructors' course, I knew I would be able to shut down during extreme pressure, and as long as I was allowed to resurface after the day's training, recharge and escape, I would survive. Yumoto Sensei had brought me here for the sole purpose of learning the ways and manners of karate and, in the wider sense, Japanese culture. This, I convinced myself, could be done gently and without undue violence.

Two hours later we arrived at a small town somewhere in Nagano, a mountainous area renowned for its winter sports and natural beauty. Called the Japanese Alps, the area is overrun with small hotels and *ryokan*, filled to the brim in the skiing season. As it was still the first week of September, the place was literally deserted. Five minutes from the station, we arrived at our *ryokan* and gathered in the largest room of the inn. I stood by as the captain shouted out orders. Several of the less-scarred individuals arranged the low-lying tables that were scattered about the place into one large coffee table going down the centre of the room. Then all forty of the Teikyo team deposited their luggage in one corner and sat around the table in traditional *seiza* position. I followed suit whilst the rice-paper doors were slid shut. Waiting in silence, I looked around the room. I made the forty-first person of the group. There were three girls and everyone was arranged by year. This was easy to tell, as the First Years, sitting at the bottom of the table, looked fresh and innocent. They even had a little puppy fat around their faces. As I moved up the table, the second and Third

Years looked a little leaner, harder and had a posture and physique that denoted years of hard training. The fourth years had an air of authority about them. Their muscles were practically popping out all over, plus they sported more scars then those of less seniority. Fresh-faced First Years looked untouched, but as the years of training increased, so too did the amount of scars: around the eyes, cheeks and mouths, their faces looked like they had been ritually tattooed or cut in some African witch-doctor tradition. However, I feared the way they got their markings was by a far more random tradition.

Suddenly, Yumoto Sensei flung open the door, as much as a sliding door can be flung, and strode in. Jumping to our feet, we all bowed and said hello. When he had sat down, so did we and what seemed to be a meeting was called to order. Yumoto Sensei went through a number of rules and regulations, which, had I listened, might have come in useful. It wasn't that I couldn't understand what was being said – I could, but it took an incredible amount of energy to listen intently for familiar words and phrases and then fill in the blanks in my mind to come up with a reasonable interpretation.

My Japanese had improved steadily over the last year. Sueki, keen to teach me as much colloquial language as he could, had quickly moved on from Japanese swear words – which amount to 'urasai da yo! (you're loud) and 'dame da yo! (that's bad) – to more useful phrases and vocabulary. I had come to understand that Japanese culture is ambiguous and adaptable, and this may stem from their language. It is sound-poor, with only fifty-two sounds to make words, whereas English has over a hundred sounds to choose from. Consequently, one word, for example, *kaeru*, can mean several things: to return home, to be able to buy, to change, a frog. When people have a conversation they are constantly hearing the words spoken, making choices out of the numerous possibilities that arise and creating a sensible interpretation of what is being said. This can seem confusing but after a while you learn to go with the flow. When Yumoto Sensei commands us to '*kaeru*' in the middle of an intensive *kumite* session, you know he isn't telling us to go home, simply directing us to change partner. The result was that I could understand about 40 per cent of what people said. This, surprisingly, is enough for a sufficient understanding of most conversations. However, the energy required to fill in the blanks is enormous and when someone is just rabbiting on about how it is vital to make sure that all slippers must be placed at exact right angles to the entrance door, I switch off. I simply sat motionless, trying to project myself out the window and far, far away. It seemed I had learnt nothing from the unfortunate incident with Shima Sensei that had started the cascade of events that brought me to this *gasshuku* in the first place. I realize now that it must have been some sort of defence mechanism, and whenever my brain became overloaded, it shut down. With a thud of the heart, I was dragged back to reality as I heard my name being called out. Looking up, I realized Yumoto Sensei was telling me to stand. Getting to my feet, he introduced me to the rest of the group and then continued by saying that I was to be treated as a first year and that I was here to study Japanese etiquette. It all sounded very cosy, in an anthropological sort of way, but I quickly learnt what being a first year really meant.

The meeting was adjourned and straight away I was being told what to do. The large room where we had all been sitting was the First Years' room. We were given five minutes to sort it out, unpack our stuff and get into the dining room to prepare dinner. I learnt early on that even the year groups had their hierarchical system, and I was at the bottom of mine. The head first year, Omura, gave out orders and they were followed immediately. I think he saw me as a hindrance rather than another hand on deck, so my orders came with a certain amount of spit and venom. We unpacked, or rather threw items of clothing into a corner, then made our way to the dining room and set about preparing dinner. Places had already been set by the kitchen staff and a lacquered tray with a large piece of bony fish had been placed on it. Our job was to go around all forty-odd places and add a bowl of rice, miso soup, a glass of tea and the assorted and, as far as Japanese cuisine is concerned, compulsory pickles, dried seaweed and sachets of seasoning that look like a cross between fish scales and dandruff. Just as we finished the preparation, the second, third and fourth years filed in and sat down. Then followed a number of men who I had never seen before, some just old and decrepit, and others who looked like killers: they fitted well into the Teikyo University hierarchical system. Taking their places at the senior end of the fourth-year table, they were obviously *O-B*. There was only one remaining empty place. Situated at the top of the senior table, the chair, no different from all the ones we were sitting on, took on an air of regality as we waited for Yumoto Sensei. Within each year there was the obvious hierarchical system, with the weakest at the bottom of the table and the strongest, the year head, at the top. Plus, with an almost pack mentality, everyone seemed to relish the pleasure of victimizing the First Years in some way or another. As in a gorilla troop, great care was taken by the juniors not to be noticed. No eye contact, no arm waving, no fast movements.

I must have come across as a simpleton. The situation was beyond what your average westerner – no matter how long they have lived in Japan – would ever experience, or would ever want to. The idea of the original *Karate Kid* film, with Mr Miyagi teaching Daniel-san how to wax on and wax off, had become a laughable cliché, because the very fact that Mr Miyagi called his protégé Daniel-san meant there was an underlining level of respect. My situation right now, in the heart of what Japanese karate truly is, was far removed from such lofty notions. I was twenty-seven years old. I was surrounded by killing machines disguised as teenagers, and I had a week-long, seven-hours-a-day excursion into hell to look forward to. No wonder I just switched off, but to the outside world I must have looked like an intellectually challenged Barney Rubble.

Yumoto Sensei arrived; we stood, said good evening. When he sat, we sat, when he ate, we ate. Since our seniors had arrived they had been barking out orders for us to follow. As it was my first day, I don't think they had quite learnt how to corrupt my name into a pronounceable form, so I simply stood by as the others had to run, fetch, bow and grovel their way around the *ryokan*, but with the seniors' mouths full of food, we were left alone. We started eating our dried salty fish and dry sticky rice. In the coming week I would become very used to not only this type of food but also my body's reaction to it. It made me retch. Gagging, I tried to force a little down as I knew the next day I would need every ounce of energy I could muster. It must have been nerves that produced this reaction, as I had had worse Japanese food than this. Having managed to eat raw chicken meat then surely this diet would give me no problem, but the pressure of the *gasshuku* was getting to me and wanting to throw up was the immediate symptom of it.

During food prep, Omura had quickly introduced me to members of our little band, so I knew the big 6'2" guy to my left was Takayama. Being young, he still carried puppy fat around the face. Not that I realized it at the time, but he must have been going through his own personal hell. He never smiled or laughed (I just thought he was someone who found the joy of life difficult to locate). Nor did he speak much, so sitting next to him during meal times wasn't going to be the highlight of my day. Seeing that I had finished eating, he turned on me and with a mixture of panic and anger whispered a command to clean my plate. I was pleased he had acknowledged my existence but shocked that I had been ordered, like an insolent child, to finish my food. This hadn't happened to me in nearly twenty years and I thought it was a bit of a joke. Explaining that I wasn't hungry only brought the attention of the other First Years. A panic seemed to sweep the table and Oyama, the only girl in our group, tried to explain that we had to finish all our food.

Later, in the privacy of our own room and out of earshot of

the dreaded *sempai*, I was told that respect must always be shown, which extended to eating all the food. Like in some nightmare prisoner-of-war camp, we had to show our gratefulness for the food by eating every last grain of rice. This was emphasized to such an extent that every member of my group told me so. But when we were still in the dining room I was unaware of the *faux pas* that I and, by association, every member of my group was about to make. Omura, with a few murmured commands, put a plan together. Under the very noses of the second and Third Years, rice, fish and pickles were quickly taken from my plate and eaten with the speed of starving men. Once the dishes were clean the group gave a united sigh, but my comrades weren't very impressed with my actions.

The meal finished, we cleared away everyone's plates, prepared the dining room for breakfast and then returned to our room. Away from the prying eyes of the seniors, everyone relaxed and set about telling me what I could and could not do in the dining room. The 'every grain of rice' epic was repeated *ad nauseam*. So too was the need to keep constant vigilance for nearly empty glasses. Like some sort of demented border patrol, we had to stay alert, stopping any glass from becoming empty. Our very lives seemed to depend on it, as if empty glasses signalled sleeper cells to reawaken and our world would be lost to fundamentalism.

We settled down for the evening. Including me, there were eight men/boys in our room. Oyama was with the two other girls on the second floor, so our room had a high-school-on-tour feel to it. The seven First Years, all eighteen years old, constantly talked about girls and drinking, but judging by what was being said they knew very little about either. I had brought two books with me, *Notes from a Small Island* by Bill Bryson and a small, self-published book that my mum had sent me called *The Leccie Man* about a guy in Liverpool who had worked for the electricity board, reading meters. After years of persuasion by his family and friends he had written down all his little anecdotes and published them for the world – or at least Liverpudlians – to enjoy. Books had become an escape, and with the prospect of training tomorrow and the hormone-driven drivel around me, I needed a little help to forget my surroundings. I started to read. Occasionally a *sempai* would burst into our room. Everyone would stand up (I was the noticeable exception) and see to his needs before attending again to whatever they were doing, but on the whole it was a good evening and I slept well.

Being kicked awake at 6:30 am by Omura is like having an alarm clock with attitude. Imagine a device that got really pissed every time you put it on snooze, until eventually it leapt from the bedside table, pulled the wires from the socket and electrocuted you out of your slumber. A gentle way to awaken compared to Omura's well-placed kicks. I rummaged around my clothes until I found my *dogi* and, still tying my belt, followed the rest of the First Years out the door. Standing in the morning sunlight, the air in Nagano was crystal clear. Having breathed Tokyo smog for several years, I was amazed at how much I appreciated clean air. Maybe it was symptomatic of the five months I had endured on the instructors' course that such a simple pleasure seemed to be heightened in contrast. Or maybe decreased pollution and purer air gave me an oxygen rush and I was simply experiencing an artificial high.

The rest of the students filed out, with Nakata arriving last. The captain then led us on a gentle jog around the town. Stopping at a small grassy area near the start of the would-be ski piste, we spent twenty minutes or so stretching and cajoling our bodies into action. This was then followed with an equally pleasant jog back to the *ryokan*. Our first training session was over. As I took off my trainers and returned to the room to change into a tracksuit, I allowed myself the slightest of hope to think that if the *gasshuku* was like this, then there would be very little to worry about. The first morning's breakfast closely resembled the first evening's dinner. Takayama, watching from his great height, tried to will every

102

food-laden chopstick-full down me. As they saw me tire, Operation Herring-Pickle was put into action and my plate was cleared. I downed my vile, cold, weak tea and waited for the rest of the group to finish theirs.

I had been in the camp for less than twenty-four hours, but already I was learning to identify the types of personalities that made up my fellow *gasshuku* -ees. Nakata, although heavily scarred under the eyes and reportedly the best fighter in the group, seemed genuinely kind and sincere. He had gone out of his way to talk to me after the morning run and I had noticed him several times give short, sharp, guttural commands to juniors, telling them to help the *gaijin* in some way or another. Mori, the vice-captain, on the other hand was in complete contrast to Nakata. He too was tough and scarred – obviously a prerequisite to make it to the top of this little pile – but I was told he lacked that little extra bit of spark that got the punch in first. He also liked bossing people about. He was only a short guy and had the temperament of a Yorkshire terrier. Takayama took a great deal of abuse from him and whatever Takayama did, Mori seemed to find fault. I am sure that deep down inside, Takayama wanted to swat him like a fly. I had recently learnt that Sueki, Koyama and Takahashi had all been vice-captains of the university in their time and I started to wonder if *almost* making it to the top gave them that little sense of insecurity. Sueki and my *sempai* had seemingly channelled that 'failure' in their lives to push themselves through the instructors' course. Mori seemed to be channelling his insecurity and anger in the direction of abusing juniors. I never liked bullies. When I was eight years old a bully in the year above me at school had picked on a number of my friends and then tried to pick on me. I had knocked him out. I was determined to show Mori how I felt.

Breakfast over, my group, like beaten wives, cleared up after their tormentors; quietly, quickly and without complaint. By the time the last chopstick was accounted for, the time was 9:15 am. Omura and the rest of the gang filed into our room, but as we

103

entered, Masaki, rushing to simultaneously take off his tracksuit top whilst putting one leg through his *dogi* bottoms, told me to hurry, we had to be at the *dojo*. Five minutes later, with only Masaki as company, I arrived to the *dojo* for the first time. It was a general-purpose sports hall with no showers, toilets or medical room, just a hall and two sinks in a small kitchen area. Quickly we brushed the room methodically up and down, disturbing a variety of insects from their night's sleep. Then we set about making the tea. A large tea urn, straight from a 1970s village fête, was filled with slightly off-colour water from the kitchen tap and to disguise any cholera, several plate-sized tea bags were dumped in and the potent mix was given a stir. The refreshment, exactly the same as at breakfast time, would be our only way of rehydration during the three-hour sessions.

Then the towels were prepared. Never, in the history of towel preparation, has any group of young men taken so much care over so little. Almost measuring out the amount of liquid, every towel was dampened through an origami-style technique of folding, dampening, wringing and then further folding, to produce the perfect wet-wipe. Then the secret ingredient was added: with the subtlest of wipes a bar of virgin white soap was passed across the glorified hankie and with an almost royal reverence, Masaki extended the finished product to within an inch of my nose.

'Perfect,' he proclaimed with a hint of pride. The ideal combination of fragrance-induced cleanliness without the soap-in-your-eyes stinging hazard had been reached. We spent the next fifteen minutes going through the other fifty towels trying to recreate the Zen-like perfection.

By 9:50 am the others had arrived and as the hands on the clock clicked to 10 am, training began. Standing in a circle, it dawned on me that our numbers had slightly swelled. What looked like more *O-B* had arrived. These were younger than the *O-B* at breakfast and as they were warming up, I feared they had come simply to re-live the chance of beating up First Years. My guts started to twist.

Whether it was the presence of more *O-B* or the fact that I was now surrounded by these monsters, the full reality of my situation hit home. As I suppressed the urge to throw up, we sat down to stretch our legs and arms. Lying on my stomach, my left then right arm were stretched, pulled and contorted into tendon-lengthening positions. Face down, hiding from my environs, I started to fall asleep. As the week progressed I would look forward to this part of the warm-up as it was a chance to hide, no matter how short a time, from reality. Hindsight has given me no further clues as to why I didn't take the easy option and just escape. I could have walked to the *ryokan*, packed my bags, got the train – I even had the ticket – returned to Tokyo and resumed my life as a carefree *gaijin*. I could have changed *dojo*, never again having to face my tormentors. However, one solid, undeniably simple and straight-forward choice is often beaten down by a multitude of half reasons, insecurities, misplaced desires, wants and needs. Fearing the re-action of Yumoto Sensei and, with Stockholm syndrome to boot, I felt I couldn't leave and let him down. I think also, somewhere in the recesses of my mind I didn't want to let myself down.

Yumoto Sensei arrived at 10.15. Pairing up, we started to do *jiyu-kumite*. With murderous speed these people, regardless of age, ability or sex, got stuck in and before I knew it, my lip was split and blood was trickling from my nose. We changed and I faced Mori. With an air of delight he quickly took me apart and seemed ready to scalp me as I lay at his feet. Fortunately the command to change was called again. This continued for twenty minutes. Sometimes I got other First Years and the odd Second Year and I managed to hold my own, but it seemed every time I turned around a Third Year, Fourth Year or an *O-B* were excitedly waiting to destroy me. It was worse than the worst of the *kenshusei* lessons and my legs and lungs were about to concede when *'Yame'* was called. Yumoto Sensei said *'K ihon'* and everyone lined up for basics. Without pausing for breath, the drills started. Up and down the *dojo*, we practised *kihon* combinations similar to the instructors' course programme, which helped me to get into the rhythm of things. But what was different was the number of people. When training at the *hombu dojo* it was very difficult to hide from one's *sempai* and *sensei* as there were only seven or eight people training, plus we were surrounded by mirrors. Here, there were forty or fifty people, no mirrors and much opportunity to hide. Obviously everyone else was also aware of this and seemed to be constantly vigilant regarding the whereabouts of Yumoto Sensei and the older *O-B*, who were assisting Yumoto Sensei. When they were near, train hard, when they were at the other side of the large *dojo*, relax and just do an energy-saving close approximation of what was being asked of us. Quickly learning from my *sempai*, I cruised through the entire hour of basics.

Kihon finished, we were given a five-minute break, a chance to stretch and re-hydrate. Correction: the Second, Third and Fourth Years were given this chance. The First Years quickly filled cups with the ubiquitous flowery tea and passed it out to all *sempai*. The higher up they were, the farther they seemed to stand from the tea urn. After thirsts had been quenched, we First Years quickly downed several cups of the vile stuff and then made our way to the edge of the *dojo* and sat in traditional *seiza* position. Lactic acid, which had slowly begun to escape from my legs during the tea run, was now trapped as we waited for the lesson to start again. I sat there with the knowledge that we had already done *kumite* and *kihon*, so the last hour or so must be reserved for *kata*.

We were told to pair up, and what followed was an hour of carefully choreographed *kumite* drills aimed at building speed, teaching distance and timing and giving me more bruises than I thought were possible. With the constant changing of partners, I started to become deeply suspicious as to why each of my new persecutors was so fresh and ready for action. Putting my all into it for the five minutes or so I had with them, they left me equally tired and sometimes as bloody, but then, with the next change, I was faced with a new, fresh-faced *sempai*. Finally I came up against Masaki.

106

I think, through our tea-making duties, we had built up somewhat of a friendship. He was a huge football fan and the night before I had induced child-at-Christmas-like excitement when I had told him I came from Liverpool. I think he saw me as his link to football trials, a chance to turn pro and ultimately his marriage to the next winner of *X-Factor*. Either way, when it came to the *kumite* drills, each of his techniques lacked the deadly element that my previous partners had displayed. In fact, the only time he did up his game was when Yumoto Sensei came close, but even then I held my own. Whilst with him, I had a chance to look around. In the *dojo*, spread out over an area that was greater than two basketball courts, were about twenty-five pairs, throwing punches and kicks to the count. Like a perverse version of synchronized swimming, everyone moved with a certain fluidity that is hardly ever seen in western *dojos*, but none of them had that murderous intent that was obviously reserved for the only *gaijin*. They were cruising through the lesson and only upped their game when Yumoto Sensei was close, or when I stood in front of them.

'Fuck you,' I muttered to them all. I pushed on and made it to the end of the session.

At one o'clock we made our way down the hill from the *dojo*. My first session was finished, but no time to celebrate as First Years hurried back to prepare lunch. Our midday meal followed the familiar pattern of dried fish, sticky rice and foul tea, but as my body was craving every possible nutrient, I gagged far less often. Lunch was followed by a thirty-minute break and everyone disappeared to their rooms. I instinctively climbed onto my futon and before my head hit the slightly lumpy, bean-filled pillow, I was asleep. Thirty seconds later – or what felt like it – Omura was kicking me awake and we made our way back up the hill. An almost identical lesson followed, but with the added delight of tube training. This type of training is designed to pinpoint weaknesses in technique. In reality it demonstrates weaknesses to one's *sempai* and they work on you... with a *shinai* – the bamboo swords used in *Kendo*. Tube training involves four or five bicycle inner tubes that have been split and tied together to make one huge elastic band. The tube is then anchored to some suitable thing or person and the other end is held by the *karate-ka*. Holding it in one's hand, punches can be practised: looping it around one's ankle, kicks can be practised, and putting it around one's waist, attacking combinations can be practised. It is the toughest form of training I know. Without tubes, in normal training, after a while the weight of one's own body (even the weight of one's sweat-drenched *dogi*) becomes unbearably heavy. Add resistance tubes to this and it is like training in thick soup. Fatigue and lactic acid hit you within minutes and like human yo-yos we pushed and were pulled up and down the hall. I left the *dojo* after three hours, exhausted, bloody and bruised.

Dinner was at 7 pm prompt. My little group had prepared everything. People were tired and apart from the occasional grunt in our direction from a *sempai*, the meal passed uneventfully. Lights out was at 10.30 pm, so we entered our room at 8 pm to be confronted with a mountain of tubes that had been used that day. Our job – a job only a first year was fit for – was to clean every inch of every tube that lay before us. Wet cloths in hand, we set about the task and finished at about 10 pm. With thirty minutes remaining, we scrambled over the road to the convenience store, bought chocolate and sugar-laced drinks and returned to our bedroom. The lights-out curfew was a formality and before the sugar rush from three KitKats had kicked in, I was asleep and dreaming of a life more ordinary.

It is difficult for me now to understand what made me get out of my futon the following morning. If ever a lie-in was called for, it was that day. From the moment we were up, *sempai* were at the door barking orders or threatening punishments for things we had forgotten to do the day before, and we hadn't even started training yet. But these post-pubescent heroes took everything without complaint, even throwing in a bit of humour for good measure. Once, after Omura (as first-year captain) had been given a particularly harsh dressing down by Mori for failing to have toothpicks at hand after a meal, Omura immediately went into a perfect impersonation of him.

'You!' as he stood in front of Masaki. 'Tell me, who has the biggest dick in all of Teikyo?'

'Oh, you of course, Mori Sempai,' Masaki.

Omura then went round to each member of our group asking other stupid questions. It was childish entertainment, but it helped get everyone through the day. The Japanese sense of humour was innocent, with a large helping of slapstick. I had watched celebrities on TV assault presenters with a slap across the face only for the studio band to instantly add the compulsory cymbal sound effect. The audiences would go mad with delight at the hilarity of such a thing. Hidden camera 'comedy' programmes were also a big hit in Japan, as were game shows that humiliated the contestants. I struggled to see the droll side of most of these shows, but as I found myself being included into the ritualistic fun-making of the *sempai*, I began to see the need for such stress outlets. Sometimes the slapstick nature of Japanese comedy seemed quite a sophisticated rebellion to hierarchy.

Each day was much the same as the last and after many sessions of trying to block attacks, bruises began to spread up my arms and legs. Like a piece of fruit that is abandoned on the kitchen table and allowed to rot, I was becoming a darker and darker shade of purple. During training, the *sempai* still seemed to step up a gear when faced with me. However, Mori was different. Obviously suffering from small-man syndrome, he was always ready to give me a little extra dig, whether it was called for or not.

In the evening we found a rhythm with the tasks. We copped on that not every tube had to be cleaned – they just had to look like they had been cleaned, so a damp cloth and a quick swipe of the hand did the trick. The process of perfectly scenting the towels was also speeded up as we found that moistening them in slightly soapy water combined the two actions. The constant washing of *sempai dogi* s was still a time-consuming burden, but we quickly had the washing-machine timing down to perfection, so even that wasn't much of a chore. Furthermore, with practice, even the laying out of the tables three times a day soon became a militaristic operation with everyone assigned a number of tasks.

This efficiency, though, left us with more time on our hands. The rest of the first years looked at porno magazines or watched TV programmes that shrilled out nonsensically. By the end of the day I had had enough of Japanese language and people and craved my English thinking time. The choice to take my particular two books was inspirational: Bill Bryson managed to conjure up images of everything British and the stories of *The Leccie Man* made me proud to be from Liverpool. In the eight days I was at the camp, I read each book three times, and the ability to transport myself from Japan to England undoubtedly saved my sanity. I hated every minute of the course and emotionally shut down far more than I had ever done in Tokyo, but at night I allowed my emotions to resurface and although I had no contact with family or friends at home, I was happy, and I no longer suffered from OCD. It was a miracle.

At the beginning of the week my main focus was getting through to Wednesday. I had been told we would have a day off, and even better, Sueki was due to arrive: a friendly face and a day of rest were just what I needed.

Wednesday dawned and it was announced that we would be climbing one of the mountains that was normally reserved for people to ski down. As a kid I had walked a great deal with my family and the prospect of climbing a hill didn't fill me with joy, but at the same time it was better than being beaten in a *dojo*. We set off, *O-B* at the front, followed by fourth years, then third, second and finally First Years, looking like a synchronized formation wing of the Ramblers' Association. As we got farther up the hill it became apparent that these young lads were not used to the idea of walking – living in Tokyo, they probably travelled everywhere by car or train. The hill definitely became a mountain and soon I started to pass Second Years, their pace roughly that of a reluctant child being dragged to the dentist. I passed the third and fourth years. By this point most of the *O-B*, with nothing to prove and a bit more common sense, had turned back. I was at the front with Mori. Not wanting to lose ground, Mori, the dark-hearted, little man, was pushing himself beyond the capabilities his little legs were designed for. I, on the other hand, was well into my stride. Unfortunately, I had no idea where I was going and decided the best plan was to stay with my hobbit guide, although at one point it did cross my mind that getting lost up here, having to spend a night and then stagger back in the morning, dehydrated and windswept, may qualify me for early release. Eventually the pack became a thin line of anxious little faces.

'Mori!' It was Nakata, shouting from well below to his vice-captain. 'Is this the right way?'

We seemed to be getting into some thick undergrowth. Boots and machetes would have seemed more suitable than the tracksuits and trainers we had brought along. As if by magic a little old man appeared. Like some clichéd guardian angel, he looked to have no reason for being on the mountain. He was in his late seventies, wore shorts and hiking boots and held a large walking stick. Mori chatted to him for a couple of minutes and then turned around to Nakata:

'We are on the wrong mountain!'

'Did you say... "wrong mountain"?' Nakata was not happy with his vice-captain, who in his bid to keep up with me, had led us the wrong way.

For me, this was the first time that not listening to what was going on had paid off. Apparently they had planned to walk up the steady slope of a beginners' piste, make their way to the café, which they had been assured was open all year round, have a drink and an ice cream and then saunter back down for lunch. What had happened was that we had spent the last two hours fighting our way through overgrown, triffid-like plants, grappling with a gradient of 2:1 and having no better view than the backside of the person in front of you.

'Did you say... "wrong mountain"?' Nakata hissed urgently. It was the first time I had seen him show any sort of temper. The effects were immediate, as Mori quickly turned to our new saviour and frantically asked for directions in rapid, panicky Japanese. Arms were pointed and directions given and Mori shouted down, in I-am-ever-so-sorry Japanese, that he now knew where he was going.

We walked for a further hour until eventually we spotted the café with all its promise of chocolate and fizzy drinks. Mori, remarkably, had managed to say not a single word to me for the whole ninety minutes I had been walking with him. Perhaps overcome with his triumphant discovery of the lost café, he raised his arm and shouted, 'There!'

'Thanks,' I said as I marched off. I had been slowing my pace to stay with him, but now I saw where I was going nothing, was going to hold me back. Leaving Mori and the rest well behind, I made it to the café a good ten minutes before them, giving me the first bit of time alone since I had landed in *gasshuku* hell. Mori arrived first, looking exhausted and deflated. I hadn't truly appreciated how much of a competition it had been for both of us, but I did allow myself a little victory smile as he stumbled through the door. It took a further forty-five minutes for everyone to arrive and I felt sorry for Oyama and Takayama who arrived last. As they sat down the whole group were told to down their Cokes and set off again.

It had taken us three hours to reach the top and it took thirty minutes to return to the *ryokan*. Everyone was exhausted, but still elated from my 'victory' and the prospect of a relaxing afternoon, I had a certain spring in my step. As we rounded the corner and headed to the *ryokan* entrance, Sueki stuck his head out the window and greeted me with the friendliest face I had seen all week, and I was happy for the first time in an eternity.

During lunch Sueki sat at the head of the senior table and so we never had chance to catch up. My fellow lackeys cleared up the *sempai* s' mess and afterwards I collapsed onto my futon, book in hand, ready to project myself back to Blighty. Masaki came over, panic on his face.

'What are you doing? We have to get to the *dojo!* Towels... make tea... clean dojo...' he continued in pidgin Japanese as he pointed at his watch. My heart sank. This was our day off! I was so mistaken. Our mammoth stroll up the hill had been our break. My legs were still shaking from that last ten-minute dash to the café. Now I was the one who looked a loser. How had I misunderstood?

We followed the ritual of preparation. The others filed in, and as Sueki arrived he came over and said he had heard I was a good climber – the first positive comment from him for a long time. Then during training, a curious thing happened: they started to ease off me. Sure, when Yumoto Sensei was passing by, everyone stepped up a gear, but during the hidden moments, the punches, kicks and little digs were far less fierce. Of course, Mori never laid off, but on the whole things became easier.

Halfway through the last hour, I paired up with Sueki. All was going well until one of the *O-B* passed by. His eyes lit up. I had seen this before, as the head-butt incident months ago was still a fresh memory. Once again things went up a gear. The attacks were coming thick and fast, but a new relaxation that I had found on the course enabled me to block the vast majority of his strikes. This only resulted in his increased frustration and, I presume, the *O-B*'s increased disgust. Eventually, Sueki tried to *ashi-bari* me: holding on, I brought him down. Outraged, Sueki carried on. Wanting to end this, I put him in a head lock and slowly applied the pressure. One thing that I surpassed Sueki on was strength. He once warned one of his *kohai* never to allow me to get hold of them, because if I did they would be dead. Slowly, as I tightened my forearm muscles and biceps, his air was cut off and Sueki began to choke. I could feel the rage in him as he fought to get free, but he knew, as

I did, that he was finished. He stopped struggling and it was over. I had beaten Sueki, a feat made all the better for doing it in front an *O-B*. I let go, thinking two victories in one day, things couldn't get any... WHACK! He had stood up and kicked me hard in the side of the head. I didn't pass out, but the *O-B* was immediately by my side. The vision in my left eye blurred and slowly darkened until I really couldn't see anything out of it. I remember being dragged to one side and then Yumoto Sensei came over.

'What happened?' He was ignoring Sueki and talked directly to the *O-B*.

I lay there whilst Yumoto Sensei gave Sueki a huge dressing-down in front of the whole class. Not worrying about my eye – although I should have been making my way to the hospital – I was happy that at least I wouldn't have to train the rest of the session.

I know Sueki so well. We are like brothers, and he is the kindest, truest friend I will ever have. I understand the forces that drive him to be one of the best in the world. That day with Teikyo and the day he head-butted me during instructors' course training represent him in a way that is far from comprehensive. From an early age he has only known the *kohai-sempai* relationship, a perfect yet flawed system. Once in it, you can never escape from its obligations but at the same time people will always be obliged to you. You must help and develop *kohai*, but will be helped and developed by *sempai*. It is a system with no beginning and no end that takes care of you as much as you must take care of it. Sueki is my *doki*, and when he hit me I am under no illusion that it was his fists and his will that were doing the damage. But it was the system he was adhering to, and not a sense of malice or sadism. Loss of face forced Sueki into a corner and he reacted the way he did. That doesn't mean I like or condone it, but I do understand it.

Unfortunately by the Thursday morning my eye had recovered and I was back training. I am sure word of the incident had done the rounds as things were noticeably better. The last three days passed by without any major injury, although the pressure was still there. By the last day I had reached my limit. The final session, Saturday afternoon, as we were warming up after the break with full speed and power *kumite*, I started to cough uncontrollably. Everyone looked round as I began hacking up a lung. My partner and I both stopped and I stood up straight trying to catch my breath. Like a scene from *The Matrix* I was completely motionless, trying to compose myself as a whirlwind of fists and feet surrounded me. Once settled, the coughing stopped and we resumed our fight, but as soon as we did, the hacking fits resumed. We stopped again, recovered, started and again the coughs returned, this time with a pronounced death rattle bad enough for Yumoto Sensei to come over for a closer inspection. For the first time since starting the instructors' course I saw a glint of kindness in him.

'It's OK. Rest off.' He said this with a hint of pride. I staggered off and sat down with a group of four or five students. They were a cross-section of years, all of whom had had to stop training due to injury. I couldn't believe I hadn't noticed them before, but it was great not to be the only one out. Then it dawned on me. I was done! Seven days of hell had come to an end and I was allowed to sit back and watch the last hour of training. The week had taken everything out of me. I had been a physical wreck throughout the days and withdrawn heavily into myself during the nights. I had been beaten and literally kicked when I was down, but I had made it. Richard Amos had left the *gasshuku* after three days and Carlos Martin, who left the course before graduation, simply refused to take part. I had become the only westerner ever to have completed a Teikyo University karate *gasshuku*.

I looked around the *dojo* and began to tick off all the guys I had managed to beat during *kumite*. Everyone had at some point over the week given me a hard time, but it was important to know I had reciprocated in some small way. First Years were tough, but I still managed to hold my own. The Second Years on the whole were the same, and I had given each one of them a wake-up call at least once. Third Years had been a little trickier, but I took great delight in the knowledge that they too, at some point over the week, had received a smack from me. The fourth years, however, were the true test. There were one or two who didn't stand out and I could quickly mark them off as having received the goods. I went through the remaining six and realized that I had whacked at least four of them, albeit to a lesser level than the lower years. It was a delight to know that the killer teenagers I had met seven days ago were just normal kids, fast and strong, but nothing I couldn't deal with.

The remaining two were Nakata and Mori. Nakata had continued with me in the vein he had started. He had been kind and considerate both inside and outside the *dojo* and was genuinely warm, allowing me to relax around him. He hadn't hit me without control once throughout the week, and I like to think I had reciprocated – in reality I doubt I would have been able to get anywhere near him. Mori, on the other hand, was the yin to Nakata's yang. For every positive of Nakata's, Mori displayed the exact opposite. Cold, inconsiderate and cruel, he had been trying to knock my teeth out all week, but the mountain climb had been a turning point for both of us. By the end of the week he no longer posed a threat during *kumite*. I broke him on the mountain. He was exhausted and defeated when he arrived at the café. He was good at karate and could move very well, but he no longer trains, and gave up shortly after he finished at Teikyo. I like to think, in some small way, I helped him make that decision.

That evening we arrived back to the *ryokan* and were greeted by mountains of beer. Dinner was wolfed down and for the first time my sticky rice and dried fish went down a treat – I never gagged once, although I still couldn't face the pickles. Our weary band of combatants flew through the dining-room-clear-away routine like a well-oiled machine and afterwards we went straight back to our room to drink away our bruises, bumps and nightmares. Half an hour and two rather large cans later, Takata, one of the more friendly of the fourth years, burst in. My comrades jumped to their feet and then nearly toppled over as several units of alcohol rushed to their young heads. Towards the end of the week I, too, had got into the habit of jumping up in a *sempai*'s presence, but not any more. My twenty-seven-year-old *kenshusei* status had been reinstated, albeit by me, and I was going to sit where I was and enjoy my beer.

'Scott-san,' I looked up as, for the first time ever, I heard a *karate-ka* use the honorific ending when addressing me, 'Would you like to come up to the fourth-year room and have a drink with us?'

'Yeah, sure.' The other First Years look on in disbelief. I stood up and walked out of the room, taking a few beers with me. It hadn't really occurred to me that each year would be having its own private party, I was just happy to be drinking. As I entered the room, Nakata stood up, empty glass in hand, ready to pour me a drink. It is a fairly well-known Japanese custom that you never pour your own beer. As your glass reaches near empty some kind soul will automatically fill it up, and often you reciprocate the favour. In a hierarchical social setting *kohai* will constantly fill *sempai* s' glasses and the only way that a *kohai*'s drink would be filled is if a *sempai* is kind enough to pay that amount of attention to their subordinate. I have often gone for hours in the hope of someone noticing my empty glass, so to have the captain waiting for me at the door with a clean empty glass in one hand and a freshly opened bottle of beer in the other was something special.

'Thank you Nakata-san.' Until that afternoon I had been calling him *sempai*, but I instinctively felt the social parameters had shifted. I took the glass and it was promptly filled. Nakata gestured to the cushion next to his, and we all sat around the low-lying table. All, except one. Mori, his back to us all, was sitting in the alcove watching TV. From the questions that started to come my way, it was obvious it had been decided to invite me up for a Q&A session. Having lived in Japan long enough to understand that perceived intrusiveness is simply a way of getting to know someone,

I happily gave out the information required, but a beer later, they had obviously exhausted the 'everything you wanted to know about a *gaijin*' category and reverted back to drinking, having small conversations with their neighbour or trying to catch a glimpse of the portable TV that Mori was hogging. This party was becoming rather dull.

'Has anyone ever played any drinking games?' I offered rather tentatively. They looked on with interest.

'I once played the Yamanote game,' said Takata from the opposite side of the room. He explained that the game involved everyone in turn naming as many of the twenty-eight stations of the Yamanote line (the train line that circumnavigates Tokyo) as possible: if you failed, you drank. It was like a train-spotter's version of 'Drink Whilst You Think' and it was agreed we should have a try. The first couple of circuits, like all drinking games, were easy, but once the large stations like Shinjuku, Shibuya and Shinagawa cropped up, people started to worry. With stations like Uguisudani and Komagome up my sleeve, I wasn't about to lose this one and the fourth years began to drink themselves under the table.

It suddenly occurred to me that when Sueki first started the course, he was such a lightweight drinker that the mere mention of alcohol used to provoke a whole range of excuses from him. These guys were exactly the same. The Yamanote game ran its course, so I suggested a follow-up game that *didn't* involve language, and set about teaching them a favourite of my university hockey club. Placing one's thumbs on one's temples whilst simultaneously waggling one's fingers, the idea is to take the thumbs off the temples and point at someone in the group. The recipient must then immediately put their thumbs on the temples and waggle their fingers. At the same time the person to the left must do the same with their right hand and the person on the right must do the same with their left hand. If there are any mistakes made by the person doing the pointing, the person being pointed at or the people either side, then the culprit must drink – seems easy, but after a few drinks things get messy.

Half an hour later there was very little point in continuing the game as they had all, except Mori, reached that point of no return. More beer was brought up. Even the fact that Yumoto Sensei was sleeping on the same floor as us didn't prevent my new party animal friends from wandering the corridors of the *ryokan* in a bid to share our happiness with all its occupants. At 2 am an *O-B* sleepily walked into the room and, without a hint of disapproval, simply said, 'Enough.'

'Osu.' The party was over. As I went to leave, everyone stood up, gave me a double-handed handshake and said goodnight. Everyone except Mori, who had sat motionless in front of the TV throughout the evening. Walking past him towards the door I leant over and said, '*Mori-san... O-yasumi.*' He looked up and grunted. Having lost respect, he wasn't going to try to claw it back by being polite. He had lost because he wanted to win. I had won by not giving up.

Tomorrow I would wake up and leave as I had arrived, a twenty-seven-year-old *kenshusei* – but so much had changed in that week. I had come closer to losing my sanity than ever before, and at times I had felt crippled, unable to deal with anything more than looking at the outside from deep within my shell. I had been beaten and bullied far beyond my capacity, but ultimately I had finished the course. I went back to Tokyo in the knowledge that I had completed something no other foreign graduate of the course had ever achieved. And if I could survive Teikyo, I could also survive the instructors' course.

Chapter Seven:

Insanity

I have just spent the night in Roppongi, the *gaijin* ghetto of Tokyo, socializing with the rich expat community: bankers, lawyers and directors, sent over from the US on lucrative contracts. The plan was to drink until dawn but at 2 am they have all decided to go home and have left me alone in the bar. I've never felt so pathetic – dumped by people that I don't really like, their lack of compassion is a reminder of how isolated I have become.

There is no question of what I have to do. I can't afford the astronomically high taxi fare home, all the trains have stopped and I don't want to drink alone in a bar for three hours until the first train leaves. I have to walk. Shibuya station is about forty-five minutes away; staggering, it should take me an hour. The first train there is at 4.30 am, and if I take my time, get some breakfast, I should be OK. I set off from the glow of Roppongi's neon into the Tokyo gloom.

Twenty minutes into the journey my mind is racing. I am cold, despite the warm autumn weather, lonely, drunk and hungover all at the same time. My mind has started playing tricks on me. I am a wreck, well beyond being broken. I give up.

Suddenly someone shouts, 'DON'T YOU DARE!'

'I can't take it,' I whimper. 'I need to go home... I am going to die here.'

'NO... YOU WILL DO IT... YOU HAVE NO CHOICE,' the voice boomed. Outraged, I continue down the road, shouting back abuse, ranting and swearing.

'YOU WILL NOT QUIT... YOU WILL DO THIS... YOU WILL NOT FUCKING MESS THIS UP!' my tormentor keeps on repeating.

I find my way to Shibuya, get a train and struggle back home. It is only when I wake up the next morning that I realize just how close I am to insanity .

On returning from the Teikyo camp I went from six hours of tough training a day to two hours, but as my memory of the camp faded, so too did my ability to relax. The enjoyment of training ebbed away. It is possible that Yumoto Sensei and Takahashi Sempai were taking it easy on me in the weeks that followed the camp, but eventually I was bound to make a vital mistake and the consequences would be brutal. But that night when I walked from Roppongi to Shibuya frightened me more than any abuse dealt out by my *sempai*, and even now I find it difficult to deal with the fact that I was walking down the street shouting to myself. I tried to dismiss it as an alcohol-fuelled manic moment, but inside I knew I was at the lowest I had ever been. What must I have looked like? Emotionally dead, I spent weekdays waiting for Friday afternoons and then weekends drunk and oblivious to my situation.

Things took a turn for the better at the end of September when Tom, a karate friend from university, arrived in Japan. During one of my earlier trips to England we had gone to a party at Ishii Sensei's home, a large and beautiful house, where the walls in some rooms were literally covered with bottles of alcohol – quite conducive to lively nights. Having travelled the world teaching karate, it had become a tradition to give Ishii Sensei bottles of spirits as a parting gift, but despite his best efforts, it was more than any one man could handle. The result was that whenever we were invited to a party it wasn't exactly a bring-a-bottle affair. On this particular evening, Ishii Sensei had lined up six different bottles of vodka that he had been given on a recent teaching tour of eastern Europe. We were blindfolded, told to take a sip and guess which country each vodka came from. Failure would result in a slap on the head and being called a 'stupid burger' (despite having spent thirty years in the UK, Ishii Sensei's English was still heavily accented). Of course everyone became horribly drunk, and towards the end of the night, after we all had unexpectedly become vodka connoisseurs, we started talking about Tom's upcoming graduation. In a moment of alcohol-induced weakness and with the temptation of easy work, high salaries and beautiful women, I persuaded him to come to Japan.

Nine months later I made my way to Saitama to greet my old friend. I clearly remember walking up the platform stairs to where I had asked him to wait and as I approached he was there, a little chubbier than I remember, but still there: a living, breathing connection to home. Joy, hope, relief. Tom, I am sure, never knew how much he helped me to stay within the realms of acceptable behaviour. At times I would irritate and upset him, but we also shared some wild and crazy times together. Tom was a first year at Keele University when I was in my fourth year. He had come to university as a *shodan* in freestyle karate – the trailer trash cousin of traditional karate. He had a lot to relearn and made the brave decision to start again at white belt, instantly gaining my respect. During university and, after I left Keele, at karate courses and Ishii Sensei's house, I got to know him well. Engaged at nineteen to a stunning older woman, he was the most unlikely of Casanovas. Slightly overweight and with a certain femininity about him, he was often mistaken for being gay, but his ability to pull women was undeniable. One of his gimmicks when on the prowl was to recognize the perfume a woman was wearing and say, 'Chanel No. 5 [or whatever]... right?' He was also a great guitarist, could sing well, loved to cook and, as a killer blow, would mention that he was a black belt at karate... by the time he had got to that point in the conversation, good looks were so far down on the girl's wish list that he could have been the elephant man and still scored.

What Tom lacked in language skills when he arrived in Japan was dwarfed into insignificance by the fact that he was a blond, blue-eyed foreigner. I rapidly became used to having to translate for him as Japanese girl after Japanese girl wanted to know his number. He had Fridays off from Navo, so at 2 pm we would meet at Ikebukuro, straight after a week of training. I would stop off at the station kiosk for beers and the weekend would begin. As 'station beers' kicked in we would make our way to Shinjuku, Shibuya or Ebisu to have dinner. Later we would bar-hop and chat up girls. The best places were *gaijin* bars, wall to wall with desperate western men who were slightly outnumbered by equally desperate Japanese women. The Japanese women only wanted one thing, to escape Japan. Speaking fluent English and often western educated, they found themselves in a society where they couldn't fulfil their potential. Parents wanted them to marry, give up work and have children. Employers expected the same and encouraged this with slower promotions and lower wages. Society cemented the whole situation by not enforcing equal-rights litigation and being apathetic to the problem. Their only hope was to marry a *gaijin* and escape to the enlightenment of the west. The *gaijin* bars were therefore fertile hunting territory and, teaming up with Tom, we had a great time. We never wanted to emulate those foreign guys who prowled the streets of Roppongi in the hope of finding naïve Japanese girls to sleep with. It was simply fun, after such a long time, to chat to and have some social interaction with women.

I was discovering areas of Tokyo that I had never seen before. In Shimbashi, despite working there for a year, I had never come across the red double-decker London bus that was parked around the corner from my old Navo school. Some eccentric guy had been over to England and bought the old-fashioned London Transport contraption, brought it back, restored it and turned it into a bar. Downstairs the seats had been taken out and the area fitted with a bar, along with stools and a small standing area. It was full of Japanese *sararimen* and office ladies. Upstairs the seats had been turned around and small tables put in to make a lounge area. It was fantastic and as we were the only *gaijin* in the place we were never short of attention. It instantly became a favourite haunt.

Another favourite was Tengu. Named after the eponymous red-faced, big-nosed character from Japanese theatre, Tengu is a chain of *izakaya* serving cheap food and even cheaper drinks. There was one near our meeting place at Ikebukuro and we would often go straight there. We became such regulars that all the staff knew us as the resident *gaijin*. Starting with a beer, we would quickly move onto grapefruit sour – drinkable and hangover-free, they were always our preferred drink. After several cheap and rather potent hits, the night seemed to follow a well-rehearsed pattern. Either girls from a neighbouring table would start talking to us, invite us to a second bar and we would end up dancing and partying the night away, or we would cut our losses at Tengu and make our way to one of the local *gaijin* bars and party there. We would continue until the last train home, where one of us would have to force the other, kicking and screaming, out of the bar and so avoid having to put in overtime to pay for a taxi ride home. Although I see the amount I drank as a function of the pressure I was under and although ultimately my behaviour would force a wedge between Tom and me, the time we had was required fun and I remember it fondly.

Inevitably, partying every weekend, I found myself a few girl-friends. I had neither the time, desire or energy to chase girls just for sex, but I did date quite a few and two in particular lasted longer than most. The first was Kumiko. A graduate of artificial intelligence from Waseda University, one of the best in Japan, she was a headstrong, beautiful and determined woman. Having studied theatre on the west coast of the US, she spoke fluent English, appeared in bilingual plays and worked for NTT, the Japanese communications giant. She had long, straight, black hair, an hour-glass figure (unusual for Japanese women) and the softest lips on earth that buckled at the sides when she laughed, revealing perfectly straight teeth (incredibly unusual for Japanese women). She combined this with a wicked sense of humour that fired a sexuality I had never known before. She enticed me more than anyone had ever done. We met at mutual friend's party and right from the beginning I was intrigued by her. She wasn't like the others. Most Japanese girls bored me with their constant search for a foreign husband before they became '*Christmas Cake.*'. They were far from subtle and really off-putting. Kumiko was different. At the party, the first time we met, she challenged every preconceived idea I had of Japanese women – she accused me of thinking she was just another desperate office lady, well past her 'perceived prime'. She was perfectly justified and walked away without even waiting for an answer. A few days later I managed to get her number from my friend, rang her and asked her out on a date. After what seemed like an eternity of pleading, she accepted and we met the following weekend.

It was the first time I had seriously dated a Japanese girl. I would meet her once during the week, she would come to where I lived, we would dine together and she would spend the night. Then at the weekend, we would meet Saturday evening, do a similar thing and I would spend the night at her apartment – seemingly a bit monotonous, but the norm in Japan. It gave a certain stability to my life. Tom was dating Kaori, a third dan from the *dojo* and we would often double-date. Life in the *dojo* was still hard, frighteningly hard, but I had something to look forward to midweek and at weekends, and it wasn't only the sex. Because Kumiko was Japanese, she didn't just understand my karate life, she accepted it. And although I wasn't going to rush into anything, I thought the relationship had possibilities. But Kumiko was thirty years

---

Christmas Cake. Japanese people often refer to women over twenty-five as leftover Christmas cake. Once past Christmas Day (the twenty-fifth) no one wants to eat them anymore!

old, and I was twenty-seven. We had been dating for three months when things started to change, and I began to understand that everything that attracted me to her was in her past. She had gone against what was expected of her and found her own path, only to return to Japan and fulfil her family's expectations – and what they wanted her to do was get married and have kids. She was looking at me with a longing that I wasn't quite ready to accept. We talked about the future and she was very open.

'I want to get married,' she would say. 'And have kids and quit work.'

'What am I supposed to do, work all day and night to support you?'

'Umm. . . yeah!' She said this without a hint of guilt.

In fact, many Japanese women leave their jobs when they marry, whether they are about to have children or not. Kumiko's expectations were no different. It came as a shock to me that this wonderful girl, with whom I was beginning to fall in love, was like so many other Japanese women. We separated, acrimoniously. I knew I could never marry her and I didn't want to waste her time. Maybe life on the course had given me a greater appreciation of my time. In the past, I had continued with relationships well past their sell-by date, and now here I was giving up a great relationship just because it wasn't going to work in some distant future. It was sad and painful.

* * *

By October I began to look forward to Christmas. Sueki had no idea when our holidays would be, so we decided that I should ask Takahashi Sempai. He was equally desperate for a break, and the prospect of as much as two weeks away from the *dojo* probably made him doubly enthusiastic to gather the information. Besides, he had a fall guy and practically pushed me into the changing rooms one day after training with the mission to find out when Christmas was coming. I faced Takahashi Sempai, shaking with nerves: this may have been the first time I had spoken to him since starting the course about anything other than asking permission to leave the *dojo*, to get a drink or to throw up. He looked at me and I felt my language skills evaporate.

'Sempai...' My mouth went dry. 'When we Christmas holiday?'

'Christmas?' he said, scowling. In non-Christian Japan, the festive season is not recognized and Christmas Day is a normal working day. Christmas Eve, on the other hand, is when young couples go out on dates, have wild times and ultimately end up at love hotels: some popular venues even have clientele queuing outside. This infamous day, far from conjuring up any Christian values, produces images of desperate young virgins standing for hours in the cold, waiting for an available, recently soiled bed to become free so they can jump into it and prove that Christmas does come once a year. Therefore, asking Takahashi Sempai when we would have Christmas holidays suddenly took on a whole new meaning. He looked at me in disgust and as his stare intensified, I started to flounder until Sueki came to my rescue. The damage had already been done, so he could safely intervene.

'*Sempai*, Scott wishes to return home to spend Christmas with his family.' Sueki spoke clearly so I could understand. 'So he needs to book a flight soon.'

Although the Japanese don't celebrate Christmas, on New Year millions of Japanese families wake before dawn on the first of January and watch the sun rise. There are also about three national holidays, so people who can resist the exhilarating sun-watching occasion often travel abroad. Consequently it is one of the busiest times for airports and travel companies and every flight is booked up months in advance. I had to act fast.

'Your only concern should be staying on the course,' Takahashi Sempai muttered as he barged past me, knocking me hard into the wall. The next day I was badly beaten.

I was inconsolable. Tom's arrival had given me enough energy

128

to last until Christmas, but if I didn't go home then I seriously thought I would die. Having Jen there last year just about got me through, but if I had to spend another Christmas Day in McDonalds eating chicken nuggets it would be the last straw. It wasn't just the instructors' course, it was Japan. I needed to leave, to re-evaluate my situation. Tokyo and Japanese culture were smothering me. Like being trapped beneath a frozen lake, I was constantly, but unsuccessfully, trying to come up for air. I was desperate, and willing to take desperate measures. During the hardest times on the course my family, in particular my mum, had become a lifeline. If I was having an easy time I would call often and chat about everything, but when I was having a hard time I didn't want to talk to anyone. I am sure my mum spent many sleepless nights waiting for me to call, and the longer I didn't call the greater her anxiety must have been. Sometimes I wanted to talk about the beatings and at other times I would not want to share it with anyone, and when she asked me how it was going I would get angry about the intrusion. I must have driven them demented.

I called my mum to tell her about the situation regarding Christmas (even as I write this I can feel myself wanting to cry). At the time I was in emotional agony – Christmas is very dear to me and I was in no state to be left alone over the holidays.

'Just come home. Book the flight,' I remember my mum saying, 'sod them and just come home.'

Obviously I couldn't go against my *sensei* and *sempai*, so a cunning plan was hatched. From the day I asked Takahashi Sempai until Christmas I never once mentioned the holidays, not even to Sueki. When it came up in conversation I just responded with the convenient '*Shou ga nai*!!', Christmas and the needs of the trou-

Shou ga nai. It means something like 'it can't be helped' and is used for the most insignificant event to major disasters. I came to see it as people really not caring what happened or how things turned out in their lives, or the lives of others.

blesome *gaijin* were so low on everyone's radar that it wasn't even given a second thought.

I had no idea when we would break for the holidays, but knew from experience that it would be around Christmas Day, perhaps Boxing Day. That year Christmas Day fell on a Monday, so I foolishly convinced myself we would finish the week before and I booked a flight for Saturday 23 December, my birthday, and waited.

Time moved slowly. Training was relentless and so were the beatings, but by the beginning of December, the month's calendar was written on the whiteboard. The last day of training would be 25 December. I couldn't believe it. We would have to come in for one day and then break until 8 January. For one day only, I would have to miss the flight. I would be not be able to see my family. I would go insane. Distraught, I called home again. My flight was booked, plans had been made, but for the sake of one day's training, it was all in jeopardy. Mum began to persuade me to come home. She knew better than I did that I was at the limit of my endurance, and over the next couple of days, she convinced me to pull a sickie. In eight months of training I had never missed one day (one of the few things for which I was respected). Sueki had had a couple of sick days and Yumoto Sensei and the rest of the *sempai* were always missing one, maybe two days a week for various reason. I had been there every day since I started. It was time to take a *zuru-yasumi* – literally a cheeky holiday.

As I got closer and closer to the twenty-third I became increasing paranoid about what would happen if they found out. So much so, that when I spoke to my family on 21 December I told them I had decided not to return home because the risk was too great. I was demented with worry. My *sempai* had infiltrated every part of my psyche and even away from the *dojo* they were influencing everything I said and thought. Paranoia is a dreadful thing. I believed they would find out no matter what measure I took, and there was no way I could logically argue myself out of the situation. Although everything was in place, my mind was racing, and

130

I honestly believed I would be discovered, beaten and thrown off the course. Mum went into overdrive. The family rallied to convince me. Regardless of the consequences, they persuaded me that it was time to come home.

After training on Friday 22 December we were told that there was no need to bring our *dogi* on the Monday as we would be finishing off the week's cleaning duties. Little did I know that the last week of training in December was dedicated to getting the *dojo* clean for the start of the New Year. All that worry and I wasn't even going to miss any training! Things seemed to be falling into place. I told Sueki that I had forgotten to pay my phone bill. Outraged, I said they had cut me off and I wouldn't be able to use my phone for maybe a week until they reconnected me. He assured me that that was quite normal. I parted with the usual, '*Shitsurei shimasu. Kaerimasu.*' ('excuse me for being rude, I am returning home') and left, grinning from ear to ear. I *was* going home, and nothing else mattered.

The next morning, after some of my English students had taken me out for my birthday, I arrived at the airport still smiling, if rather hungover. The immigration lady took my passport, looked at it and then gave me a long stare. I thought she wasn't going to let me out of the country, but with a smile she wished me happy birthday and handed the passport back. I could have kissed her, but instead opted for the more usual '*arigato*' and made a dash for the plane.

Safely back in England, at 3 am GMT, Christmas morning, I called the *dojo*. Again drawing on my unexpected acting skills, I muttered something about food poisoning and told Sueki that I would not be there. He told me that no one else would be coming to the *dojo* either, and we had been left to do all the cleaning. Guiltily, I said I was sorry that I couldn't help, and then said I had to go and throw up. My poor friend never questioned me once. To him, the twenty-fifth was just another normal day and he never once thought I was pulling a *zuru-yasumi*, let alone calling from the UK. Tom, who was the only one who knew I had returned to England, rang to say that he had gone to the end of year party: all the *dojo* students were asking Takahashi Sempai where I was. With delight, Tom told me that Takahashi was making fun of me, telling the whole of the *hombu* that I was at home in bed, vomiting as a result of some dodgy *izakaya* I had visited. Everyone had bought the story. I could sit back and relax for a ten-day stress-free holiday.

I distinctly remember arriving home the evening of my birthday. It was dark and damp and I took a deep breath. The air seemed so much fresher than Tokyo, but even better, I could smell the moisture. Having been used to hot humid summers and cold dry winters, the dampness of an English December was sublime. The smell brought back a thousand memories of every Christmas I had ever had and I walked into my parents' house like I was five years old, alive with anticipation. Over the ten days I completely relaxed, and sleeping became a pleasure: I never had nightmares and I could look forward to waking up. Eating meals without having to rush in anticipation of an English student arriving at the door made every mouthful more gratifying. I was surrounded by love from my family and friends. No one mentioned Japan and it felt like I had never been away, nor would I ever have to go back. I walked about feeling healthy and energetic. In essence, I had come back to life.

I returned to Japan on 2 January and on the plane made a vow to reduce the level of OCD. The list of things I was doing had grown over the year and reached a ridiculous level. So, from 8 January I abandoned everything except the time I got up, the trains I took and the seats that I sat in. I started the New Year with renewed vigour. None of my *sempai* ever found out about my trip home. That little secret got me through many hard training sessions, and so I started the second year of the course with what I believed was enough energy to see it through to the end.

Chapter Eight:

Tick-Tock

As I finish another week of training I make my way to Ikebukuro. In a bid to stop myself drinking, I have decided to better myself, and that's why I am looking into the eyes of my gorgeous 'language exchange' partner. We will speak English for an hour and follow that with a similar hour of Japanese. To improve my language skills I am forcing myself to sit in a trendy café, drink tea and ogle this beauty. As the second hour goes by I start to understand why the language exchange system is often mistaken for blind dating for wimps and Tom's insistence that it should be renamed 'fluid exchange' creeps into my thoughts.

I am trying to reconcile the fact that Japanese has no future tense and never uses pronouns with my desire to ask her, 'Where shall we meet next week?' As my mind struggles with the complex syntax, the baggy skin just below my left eye starts to twitch.

It is twitching again... and again, like the last death throes of a hooked fish. I put my hand up to see what all the commotion is and feel the loose skin convulsing to the rhythm of my increasing heart beat. Rubbing it, as if to massage away the devil within, I catch my stunning partner eyeing me with a certain trepidation. It seems my idiosyncratic spasm is here to stay and I spend the rest of the hour facing side on to her, talking from the corner of my mouth. It is dawning on me that although I have given up most of the outward signs of lunacy and brought my OCD under control, the pressure from the course has to be released through the slack skin beneath my eye. Just when I think all is going well, my body has found a new way to remind me that I am far from the finish line.

Returning invigorated from the UK at the beginning of January, it soon dawned on me that I wasn't even halfway through the course, and wouldn't be for another four months. No one ever suspected that I had been away, but I struggled to accept that although returning home for Christmas was for me a major personal triumph, for the others it had been just another day.

The daily grind began again, but this time without the comfort of OCD. Now I understood how that facial tick, which started after a particularly tough week, was directly related to the abandonment of my OCD routine. So as I sat trying to flirt in Japanese, the tick was born and stayed with me for many months. It wasn't a constant feature, but every time my stress levels rose it triggered a visual aide-memoire that told me I was at the limit of my endurance.

And so the beatings continued. But they were becoming more infrequent, and I no longer fell into my futon in the evenings covered in cuts and bruises. In spite of this, the fear never eased. I heard that the Chinese define terrorism as 'kill one, scare a thousand'. Walking to the *dojo* every morning trying to calculate the odds of receiving a thrashing, agonizing over every interaction I had had with my *sempai* the previous day, was psychologically exhausting.

At some point I would be beaten again and as the length of time from the last pounding grew, the pressure began to mount. Eventually I would be knocked around for some instantly forgettable reason, and it would almost be cathartic – I could enjoy a few days, maybe a few weeks before I would have to face the same ordeal again. The pain itself was fleeting, but the thought of it, the waiting for it, that was the difficult part. That was the terrorist element of it all.

By the end of February, things were changing. Takahashi Sem-

134

pai had, for many years, suffered from a calcification of his right elbow, which had set in during his time as *kenshusei*. Having trained so hard and punched so many times, the constant jolting of the elbow had caused it to seize up. Karate technique is designed to maximize the body's potential, and the *karate-ka* of today are metaphorically standing on the shoulders of past masters. Previous *sensei* s' diligent study of body movement and karate technique has helped develop the art, making today's technique almost unrecognizable to the original form. (Like comparing a vintage car to the latest Japanese import, everyone wants to think the classic is superior, but in almost every measurable way the modern production car outperforms its predecessor.) But the slightest flaw in technique, a repetition of a movement, for example, can have devastating consequences, destroying joints, cartilage or ligaments over the years. Takahashi Sempai, despite being technically superb, had suffered from a slight flick of his right elbow when he punched and was now paying the price. The only solution was an operation – his third – to remove the unwanted calcium deposits, freeing up of the joint. The operation would be followed by three months of physiotherapy and only light training. This was the best news I had had all year. My tormentor would be gone for three days a week doing physiotherapy and his two days at the *dojo* would not involve hard training, which meant no *kumite* with him. If he wasn't able to carry out his bully duties, my time in the *dojo* would be fear-free.

Over the past year, the passion and love I had for karate had slowly withered. The only time I took pleasure in it was on the very rare occasions that I was allowed to teach, but with Takahashi Sempai out of commission there were a number of changes. The Friday evening class, which had often been taught by Takahashi Sempai, needed to be filled. Sueki was the obvious choice, but he already taught at one of Teikyo University's rich *O-B dojo*, where he was paid a ridiculous amount to teach five-year-olds the difference between left and right. So I was drafted in as unpaid, unwanted help. Sometimes I would teach all three classes, sometimes I would teach just one or two, before Yamada Sempai would arrive and take over. It was actually his slot, but often he didn't make it because he couldn't be arsed.

Despite working for nothing and without any thanks, I loved being back in the *dojo* on my terms and quickly took advantage of the situation. Most of the students were used to the Japanese method of teaching – basically calling out a technique and then counting and drilling them into the ground. Being western, I liked to teach something when I was up in front, and gradually the lessons filled up with *gaijin* students and English-speaking Japanese students. Traditionally a quiet time at the *dojo*, I managed to draw a decent crowd to the early evening Friday slot, and once the rest of the *dojo* found out I could teach reasonably well in Japanese, others came along for the ride.

Being in front of the *dojo*, showing technique in a relaxed manner was an eye opener. I remember doing *kumite* one evening and pairing up with a senior. A year ago I called him *sempai* (and still did out of politeness) but he was now calling me *sensei*. A year ago we would often match each other in strength, speed and determination; I now found it easy to dominate the fight, never once feeling under pressure. I could finally see the improvements my friends had been insisting on for the last few months. I rediscovered my enthusiasm for the art. At the same time we had two additions to the *dojo* line up: two new *kenshusei*, two new *kohai*, people who called us *sempai* and looked to us for guidance and advice, Juan and Kawada.

I already knew Kawada. He was the captain of Teikyo University when Sueki was vice-captain, but the year previous had chosen to pursue a career working in an office of a Teikyo *O-B*. (Good students of Teikyo can often wangle their way into one or other of the companies that their *sempai* have built up over the years. The *sempai*, the ones with a bit of business knowledge, take in these recent graduates and try to educate them to the ways of the real world.) After four years doing nothing but karate, these kids are often hapless. Unable to relate to other people without knowing whether they are *sempai* or *kohai*, adjustment to normality is often hard. The result is that they are taken in, given a salary and will, it is hoped, eventually find a role in the company. To be fair to Kawada, he had a wife and baby and to continue along the karate path wasn't so desirable for his family. However, after a year of having his energy sucked out of his eyeballs by fluorescent lighting, he decided to return to karate full time.

Kawada had never stopped training and was already a well-respected and valuable member of the all-styles national team. One of the best fighters in the country, possibly the world, he was an obvious choice for *kenshusei* and I am sure Yumoto Sensei actively pursed him, so much so that he was given huge concessions. The deal was struck and he was allowed to continue working at his old company and still draw the same salary. His schedule was that on Mondays, Wednesdays and Fridays he would come to the *dojo*, train and then make his way to the office and work from 3 pm to 5 pm. The remaining two days he didn't come to the *dojo*, he just did a normal day's work, which, he once told me, consisted of him telephoning the odd customer and making paper aeroplanes. He was a hobby *kenshusei*.

Sueki and Kawada were best friends, having been through four years of Teikyo together. I can't deny that his arrival caused a certain jealousy, but Kawada's charm and humour quickly won me over. His karate was strong and fast. I thought he just had the edge on Sueki, but for some reason I handled him better than anyone else. Having had seriously savage beatings from Takahashi and, to a certain extent, Sueki, my natural reaction when fighting them was to tense up. This reduced my speed, timing and ability to dominate. Kawada posed none of these problems. I was calm and relaxed when fighting him and I am sure he respected me – always a good thing in a partner. Moving more freely, I was finally putting into practice all the things that had been forcibly drilled into me for the last year. He was a pleasure to train with and I was glad to have him around.

Juan was different. A Mexican who had come over at the beginning of February and taken a short cut onto the course, he was technically very good and had competed in central and north America, winning many major tournaments. At twenty-four he was already a professional instructor in Lima with his own *dojo* and over a hundred students. He had then made the brave decision to leave his family and fiancée to do the course. He was being funded by his students at home (whom his senior grades had agreed to teach for the years he had to be away) so he had no financial worries and was looking forward to making a success of himself in Japan. But he got the shock of his life when he started the course, as his first mistake had been to listen to his instructor in Peru. His instructor had never done the course, never trained seriously in Japan and knew nothing of the etiquette and procedures surrounding the course. He was sending his best lamb to the slaughter...

Apparently Juan's *sensei* was an old student and friend of Taguchi Sensei and had given Juan a letter with the express orders to hand it directly to him. Like in a scene from some bad martial-arts movie, Juan made his way to Taguchi Sensei's office and handed over the letter. It asked him to take this student and allow him onto the course. Taguchi Sensei, knowing Juan's instructor, agreed. However, Taguchi Sensei didn't teach the *kenshusei*, Yumoto Sensei did. Juan turned up to the *dojo* virtually uninvited and unwanted. Of course Yumoto Sensei was told he would be on the course, but none of us was happy that he would be there, including me. I had spent three years training, never missing a class, in order to build up the trust of my *sempai* and *sensei* before I was *invited* on the course, and even then I had to fight tooth and nail to stay. Juan had landed in Tokyo, his Mexican instructor had pulled a few strings and he was admitted. Life was never going to be easy for him. Maybe he had images of us standing around as Yumoto Sensei lectured on the importance of channelling energy when executing a technique. Maybe he harboured ideas of us slowly delivering a reverse punch as Takahashi Sempai micro-adjusted our fist position. Maybe he thought that the course was the perfect circumstance to nurture a young *karate-ka* and build him into the perfect *sensei*. Whatever he thought, he was wrong, and he paid dearly for it.

When I first started the course I was numb to what was happening and the pressure built up for some time before taking its toll. With Juan it was immediate. As a devout Catholic, he quickly turned to the Bible. Before training I would find him in the changing room reading the good book, looking for inspiration, guidance... something to help him get through the next two hours. It would have been more help if he had brought the Bible into the *dojo* and used it to deflect assaults. Instead, reading the Bible became his form of OCD. I have never seen anyone change so radically, so quickly. Jolly and friendly only weeks before, he become morose and depressed and eventually withdrew entirely into himself. After training sessions I would often spend hours talking to him about his ordeal. He would repeat the same questions, unable to grasp why they were trying to hit him, why they didn't like him, why he wasn't the best in the *dojo*. One day he pulled me aside.

'I have brought a calendar,' he confided. 'If I have a good day I cross it off with a blue pen, if I have a bad day I use a red pen.'

'OK...' I didn't really know where this was going.

'They are mostly red days.' He was trembling as he said it. The course was all about being able to handle the pressure. He was never giving his mind a break, with the constant remainder of the red days looking at him. I had a calendar too. It was a day-to-day tear-away type with a joke on each page. Once a new day arrived I tore the previous day away and never thought about it again – the small things help a lot!

One night, shortly after the new students' arrival, we went drinking with Takahashi and Yamada Sempai. Sueki, Kawada and myself were *osu* -ing and bowing to our *sempai*'s every grunt and cough. We did what any good *kohai* would do; pour drinks, order food and so on, and they reciprocated by paying for everything and chatting to us quite pleasantly. I was having a great time. Kawada insisted that he poured my drinks and I plied him with more beer than he could handle. Takahashi Sempai came and sat next to me. He told me that before starting *kenshusei* he had been a high-school teacher. I asked him what he taught and he rather embarrassingly told me it had been English. Spurred on by Dutch courage, he started talking a language I had never heard before, but he assured me it was *engurishu*. I never argued, but it was good to see the human side of him. He had a great sense of humour and for the first time he was prepared to share it with me.

Despite being almost invisible, Juan was also there. He refused to drink. Apparently he never drank, but if ever there was a good time to start, it was now.

'*Hai, dozo...*' Yamada Sempai offered him a drink.

'No thank you,' he replied in English. This didn't go down well. In Takahashi and Yamada's eyes it was simply rude. The smallest of sips would have sufficed. Had Juan spent any time in Japan before he started the course, he would have realized that. No one was impressed and Juan's days were numbered.

Everyone except Juan had a great time that night, and the following week I walked to the *dojo* with a spring in my step. Not only did I have *kohai*, not only was I on the teaching schedule, not only was Takahashi Sempai out of action, but they had also started being kind to me. I had broken the back of this *kenshusei* game. That day, Yumoto Sensei felt like doing a spot of *kumite* and we spent almost the whole lesson trying to flatten each other with various drills. Takahashi, unable to take part, prowled the *dojo*. Yumoto Sensei barked out orders. After ninety minutes Yumoto Sensei took offence at one of my combinations – apparently my footwork lacked flair. As I was no Fred Astaire, especially with the ugly blood blister that was developing on my big toe, Takahashi Sempai was given the order to 'sort me out'. Yumoto Sensei watched Sueki destroy Juan, whilst Takahashi Sempai kicked me into touch. I repeated the combination ad nauseum. The night of *engurishu* was a distant memory as my blister broke and my footmarks left a bloody waltz-step pattern on the floor.

Takahashi, still unimpressed, came up and demanded that I knock Kawada down, insisting that this could only be done with a quick one-two shuffle. I tried again and returned to my mark to be met by a dissatisfied face. WHACK! With his good arm, Takahashi Sempai dropped me with a solid punch to the chin. I fell at his feet, a mixture of stars and blood floating before my eyes. The next thing I remember was a sharp kick to the ribs, followed by a command to get up and do it again. I was exhausted, but I had to comply or face the torment of the one-armed nemesis. I repeated the crazy tango. Fear is a great motivator and although I didn't manage to knock Kawada's teeth down his neck – which is just as well, as he only had about three left – I did earn a satisfied huff from Takahashi Sempai.

Looking back I can see why Takahashi Sempai did that to me. We were trying to be the best in the world, which could only be done by training harder than anyone else in the world. After that frightening incident I knew that I could always find more in myself and the scar that developed at the corner of my mouth from the punch was an enduring reminder of this. Takahashi continued to be friendly outside the *dojo* and inside he began to take a particular interest in my development. Often, unfortunately, that interest involved someone beating me up. To the untrained eye it may have looked no different from the beating I had received from him over the previous years, but there was a subtle change in his attitude and it made the blows easier to take.

As the weeks progressed, the new *kohai* were taking a lot of abuse. Juan and Kawada began their *kenshusei* training at the beginning of March. The start time for a new intake is the beginning of April and I felt sorry for them that they had to do a month more than anyone else. The new *kenshusei* test was scheduled for

141

Sunday 1 April, but two weeks into training Sueki landed a perfect *mawashi-geri* straight to the side of Juan's head. It cracked one of the vertebrae in his neck and he spent the last two weeks of March watching from the side-lines. My lasting memory of Juan is of him walking about the *dojo* with all the worry of the world on his shoulders and a permanently cricked neck. I also remember thinking that he was a lucky bastard and wishing that I was injured and didn't have to train.

On the morning of the test, Juan turned up late. Obviously he didn't have to take the test, but he still had to be there. Senior JKS instructors were ready for the bloodbath, and Sueki and I were busy serving tea. Juan came over and dragged me into the changing rooms.

'Can you translate for me?' he asked nodding in the direction of Yumoto Sensei.

'Yeah, sure. What's wrong?' I asked.

'I quit.'

I looked on amazed. He had only done two weeks. As I stumbled out of the changing room in shock, he was busy packing up his things from his locker and followed me out, ready to confront his tormentors. I pulled Yumoto Sensei to one side and, with Juan shaking next to me, explained the situation. Yumoto Sensei suddenly became human.

'I understand,' he smiled, shaking Juan's hand. 'Remember, you are welcome to train in regular classes anytime.' With that, Juan left the *dojo* and never returned. The last I heard he was back in Peru, teaching full time, promoting himself as a Japanese-trained instructor and attacking the instructors' course as a barbaric, antiquated form of training that didn't produce results.

I was still sorry to see him go, as I drew strength from having another *gaijin* there – plus, I was now the weakest link once again. Takahashi Sempai, rather cruelly I felt, asked me when I would be quitting, the implication being that this was what *gaijin* did, quit. I refused to answer him, but as I left the *dojo,* Shima Sempai

142

came up to me and remarked that I was the only *gaijin* now and finished it off with a '*gambatte ne.*'. It was heartfelt and more than I expected.

A month later Kawada dropped out. The three days a week for him was just too much. Originally from Kyushu, the southern island, he returned home with his family and the last I heard he was washing cars. It was a complete waste of karate talent and I am sure he would still be training if he hadn't been pushed so hard. Remarkably, Kawada quitting never raised an eyebrow amongst the *hombu dojo* teaching staff, whereas when Juan finished it was the natural conclusion of *gaijin* behaviour. They derided and ridiculed him as a snivelling, weak idiot who didn't deserve to wear a black belt, but Kawada was different.

'He made the choice for his family, for his future, for the greater good...'

'He is a good man who took care of his family...'

It was all bollocks. I don't doubt for a second that Kawada took care of his family, but they played no part in his decision to leave *kenshusei*. He had simply had enough. However, Yumoto Sensei and our *sempai* decided to put another spin on the whole affair, showing the Japanese ability to bend and corrupt their own code of conduct and obligation when it suits their needs. The two differing reactions to Juan and Kawada were unfair and racist.

Racism wasn't only practised by my seniors. By late May my classes were becoming ever more popular, but one week I was told I was no longer needed to teach.

Takahashi Sempai was in recovery and Yamada Sempai was still skiving. I was simply given the boot. Shima Sempai was drafted in and on occasions Yumoto Sensei took over – essentially, anyone except for me. Apparently one of the *hombu dojo* students had made a complaint. It transpired that one night, after my class, a few of us had gone out for a drink to a local *izakaya*. We

---

Gambatte ne. Try hard! Try your best! It is a phrase that is often used and the nuance, in this case, was that Shima Sempai was worried about me.

did this quite often, so I can never be sure when this 'incident' was supposed to have happened. Tamata-san, one of the senior members of the *dojo*, was with us. It was alleged that after a few *dai-jokki* – the very large beers common in Japan, like weight-lifting for alcoholics - I drunkenly referred to Tamata without the honorific *san*. I cannot remember doing this, but do admit it may have been possible. But Tamata-san was my friend: he spoke perfect English and forgave any language gaffe I made (which were frequent and, to him, hilarious). I knew it wasn't him who had spoken to Yumoto Sensei.

The result was that I was banned from teaching for nearly a year, but the really upsetting aspect is that Yumoto Sensei never supported me. He immediately took the preposterous student's side, and I was barred from the one thing I enjoyed. And if that wasn't enough, Yumoto Sensei never explained the reason – I found out because Sueki had overheard Takahashi Sempai and Yumoto Sensei talking. They felt like they had no choice but to stop me from teaching, although they knew I wasn't the rude barbarian the complaint had made me out to be. That is maybe why they didn't have the courtesy or courage to tell me to my face. The whole incident still angers me today.

The other teaching part of my life, the English conversation lessons, was equally unsatisfactory. I was still managing to maintain an adequate number of students (which barely paid the rent) but the repetition of pidgin English phrases and asking 'What have you done this week?' was tiresome. Often my students were dispassionate and bland, unwilling to take life by the horns. I did have livelier students, but they were studying for a purpose and never stayed very long.

In mid-spring, after a typically tough training session, I returned home to teach my 3 pm class. That day Takahashi Sempai had managed, with a punch, to force one of my incisors through my skin below my lower lip. I thought I had Polyfilla-ed the gap before leaving the *dojo* and returned home to start my working day. At the end of my first English class, my student left and I went the toilet before my 4 pm arrived. To my horror blood had oozed out and coagulated in my goatee beard. I looked like I had been out for a night on the town with Dracula, but my student had sat passively throughout my bloody outpouring. He had said nothing – maybe through politeness, maybe through no real care what I did, but either way this episode didn't help my loneliness and detachment.

My one saviour was Hiro. He was the local dentist and wanted to study English so that he could travel to America and continue his studies in orthodontics. Every Monday and Wednesday evening he would come round for a two-hour class. He was rich and successful and a couple of years older than me, but unlike many of the suits I taught, Hiro was amusing, lively and lived for the moment. He was already one of the top dentists in Tokyo, but his need to better himself was taking him away from his fiancée and practice, as he was planning to spend three years in America. After one of our first lessons he left the house and I had followed him out to get to the shops in time to buy dinner. He was still outside and we started chatting as we walked towards the station. I explained I hadn't eaten dinner yet and before I could protest I was ushered into one of the best *izakaya* in the area. We immediately hit it off and from then on I had dinner with him twice a week for nearly a year and a half. At first he would insist on paying for everything, but before long I forced him to allow me to pay on occasion. He was so thoughtful that when it was my turn to pay we would go to the local chain *izakaya* and when on his dime, we would check out some speciality cuisine or renowned restaurant.

Hiro also liked a drink and as I didn't drink during the week we often met up at weekends. Tom often came along and before long the three of us became very close. Tom would meet Hiro on a Thursday afternoon for a language exchange lesson, then I would meet them in the evening for food and, as time went on, I would allow myself a drink or two. It was a thankful respite. Hiro was the one student I looked forward to teaching and he became a life-long friend. He understood my situation, never asked me stupid questions and I was comfortable in his presence. But despite the friendship with Hiro, the summer months did not bode well. The *kohai* had quit, the heat was approaching, my teaching duties had been taken away and Takahashi Sempai was back. Nothing had changed.

Chapter Nine:

Once More, For Old Times' Sake!

Every *kenshusei* receives a bad beating during the summer of their second year. I had always known this from when Richard Amos spoke of his days on the instructors' course. No one else talked about their time on the course, but Richard, being English, never went in for the secret-society crap that the Japanese did. Before he left in 1999 we often went out drinking after training and he would occasionally drip-feed us stories of the rough old days at the *Hoitsugan* and his time as *kenshusei*. He once mentioned the final big one; the beating he got during the summer of the second year. He still had a major scar over his left eye, the result of a punch by Yumoto Sensei, but added that after this particular thrashing he was left alone. He had returned the following day, bandaged like a mummy but ready to train. With a sniff of recognition, they let him onto the dojo floor and from then on gave him the respect he obviously deserved. But why bother giving him the worst beating near the end of the course, rather than at the beginning? Surely the first day would have been more beneficial?

By the end of June I had somehow convinced myself that I wouldn't be receiving this judgement. I allowed myself to be-

---

Hoitsugan. Infamous in the karate world, students from all over were allowed to stay in dormitories at the Hoitsugan dojo as long as they train daily there and at the hombu dojo – like a cross between a youth hostel and prisoner-of-war camp.

lieve what I had suffered over the past eighteen months was far more than Richard had, or any of the other *kenshusei* before me, for that matter. Yumoto Sensei was older and more compassionate. He had surely seen the folly of past beatings and decided that this new generation of *kenshusei* would be spared such meaningless thrashings. As one gets older, I persuaded myself, life has a habit of replacing fire and passion in the stomach with grey hair on the head... I was hoping Yumoto Sensei was no exception, but I was fooling myself. I should have known that Yumoto Sensei, just like Taguchi Sensei when he turned up to the dojo to see the bloodbaths masquerading as *kenshusei* tests, was far from losing his passion and fire for karate, or for the stringent and severe methods of the instructors' course.

It was an incredibly hot day at the end of June. The humidity had kicked in, and as usual Takahashi Sempai had just flicked off the air-conditioning – the claim that the cold air hurt his throat was neither convincing nor worthy of him. Training started, as usual, with basics in front of the mirror. *Kumite* drills followed, again facing the mirror. This was, I was told, to help us see our mistakes and correct them. I suspected the truth was that it was the *sempai*'s and *sensei*'s job to correct us, however begrudgingly. So that they didn't have to walk around the *dojo*, scrutinizing us, disrupting their own workout, they would face the mirror, enabling them to train and at the same time check us for our appalling and inexcusable technical blunders.

At the end of a rather long hour of these basics, Yumoto Sensei took exception to the way I was doing a certain combination: my *yori-ashi* – the way I slid across the floor - was not up to scratch. The class was stopped as I was made to do it again. Despite the support of the home crowd (Sueki) my execution was excruciatingly bad. Yumoto Sensei walked off in a huff and told Takahashi Sempai to sort it out. Or was it 'sort him out'... I was about to find out it was the latter.

Sueki stood in front of me with a focus pad, acting as a target

148

for my one-two combinations. Takahashi Sempai, after telling me to use tubing whilst repeating this technique, stood behind me with a *shinai*. Sueki counted to a hundred and with every grunt from my *doki* I lurched forward, trying to make it to the focus pad. As I was catapulted back to the start point by the tubing, Takahashi Sempai told me how slow/weak/foreign I was and whacked me on the backside with the *shinai*. After a hundred I was dissolving into a puddle of my own sweat. Yumoto Sensei had long gone home and I was left alone in the *dojo* with just Takahashi and Sueki. Sueki remained impassive, but Takahashi seemed to be getting increasingly into this new and delightful way of facilitating my improvement in karate. The last one completed, Takahashi Sempai told me to take off the tubing. I was glad to get them off and I put them to one side when I heard Takahashi Sempai say, 'OK, one more time.' Sueki counted, and I remember thinking there was no need to count for just one combination – but he never stopped barking at me and it dawned on me that I had a further hundred to do. This time it was without the tubes. As before, the *shinai* continued to knead my buttocks.

The second set of a hundred over, Takahashi Sempai looked pleased. I didn't know whether his pleasure derived from my improvement of technique or my physical and mental deterioration. However, he uttered the magical '*yame*' and I thought it was all over. In fact, we had finally come to the main event. He told us to pair up. I was exhausted. Sueki, meanwhile, had been standing around for the last thirty minutes whilst I was being tenderized. Fresh as a daisy, he lurched at me: this was far beyond the *kumite* we normally practised. I had learnt to recognize the change that came over Sueki's face when he disconnected his brain from his hands. Like a computerized weapon that has just blown a few vital safety circuits, Sueki became completely removed from his surroundings. Head down, his target in sight, he became an unstoppable killing machine.

Fists whizzed pass my ear with alarming power. After the

fourth or fifth near miss, he landed one, which knocked me flying. I saw it coming but was unable to get out the way. (I had been in a car crash a number of years earlier, ironically with Ishii Sensei. I think it was symbolic of how our relationship ended up. During the crash time really did slow down, and I remember every detail of the gut-wrenching five seconds it took for the car to flip over.) Because my brain was processing so much more information so much more quickly, time seemed to pass more slowly. For the second time in my life I was experiencing the same phenomenon. Sueki came in with a one-two combination, the very one that had started this unfortunate chain of events. I blocked the first one, but as the second came in I instinctively blocked what I thought the course of the punch would be. But this one, uncharacteristically for a karate punch, came over the top like a mad bar-brawl swing. It landed solidly on my cheek and I actually felt Sueki's knuckles sink into my cheekbone. I was powerless, helpless, as if swimming in shark-infested treacle, unable to escape.

This was crunch time, literally. Sueki came in hard again and the fight continued, maybe for another twenty minutes. Every time Sueki eased up, deciding that I had had enough, Takahashi stepped in and berated him, telling him to fight harder. By the end blood was pouring from my face. I still had all my teeth, but the inside of my mouth was in tatters, mangled where teeth and fist had collided. I lay on the ground. My various internal organs felt like they had been lashed to cattle and the ranch hand had just let off his Colt 45 to scatter them across the prairie. I coughed up blood, watching it spatter across the *dojo* floor.

'You should have more respect for the floor and not make it dirty.' Takahashi Sempai kicked me in disgust. He turned to Sueki and started giving him pointers about his fighting style. Bleeding on the *dojo* floor and gasping for air at his feet, I was the one who needed advice. I was the one who needed help, in so many ways.

After a while Takahashi Sempai went off and Sueki picked me up, carried me into the toilet and cleaned off the blood. He looked

150

at me as if he were waking from a coma, unsure of what had just happened. I thought a great deal of Sueki, so even in my pulped condition I worried about him. How could he allow himself to be so controlled that he would beat me up? No matter how far I had allowed myself to fall, Sueki was in much deeper. Maybe he always would be. As I left the *dojo* that day, my mouth full of the human Polyfilla, it was with mixed emotions. I knew this had been coming and I was glad it was over. Looking back it doesn't seem so bad, but time has a way of eroding the sharp edges of memories. I was surprised I had received the beating from Sueki but I harboured no hard feelings towards him. I worried for my *doki*. He was constantly under the control of his *sempai*, and after the beating the best he could allow himself to do by way of apology was to fix me up in a bid for damage limitation.

What did surprise me was that the beating had not been meted out by Takahashi. For the past eighteen months he had never been less than eager to give me a hard time, so it came as a surprise that he had chosen Sueki. It was undeniably his choice, so something had changed from the beginning to the end of June. I had done a demonstration with him at a regional competition the week before the beating. *Hombu dojo* instructors are regularly invited to regional events to teach, referee or perform a demonstration. They are guest stars at the event and it is a way for local affiliates to pay respect to the JKS and a little money to *hombu dojo sensei*. I had then gone on to referee, seemingly with a modicum of competence. Senior instructors of the area had commented to Takahashi Sempai afterwards that the demonstration had been a huge success and, in front of me, they had congratulated him – not me – on my improvement at karate. It was the first time I had been accepted by the JKS at large as a *hombu dojo sensei* and it must have pleased Takahashi Sempai or at least made him re-evaluate his opinion of me. We had been out drinking together that evening, just the two of us, and far from being stern and overly *sempai* -ish, he had been open and friendly. The next day I never made the mistake of thinking that our friendship spilt over to the *dojo*. I understood my position in the group and I was willing to stay within those boundaries. This had been a turning point for me and for the perception that people, Takahashi Sempai in particular, had of me. I guess it resulted in Sueki being given the dreadful task. Maybe Takahashi couldn't bring himself to do it. It may have been simpler for Takahashi Sempai to accept me and therefore not give me the beating. But the rules of the course hadn't changed since its conception, and it certainly wasn't going to change because the *gaijin* made good.

Fortunately, that was it. I knew I had been through the worst. From then on I was determined to start enjoying my life. In mid July I told Yumoto Sensei that my grandfather had died, missing out the part that he had died in 1986. Thank God the Japanese language has no present perfect tense! I revisited the fear-induced school of acting – previously used in such classics as *Food Poisoning at Christmas* – and, on the brink of tears, explained that I must return to the UK at once for the funeral. I may be gone a week.

'Were you close to your grandfather?' Yumoto Sensei asked. Once I had assured him that we had spent many a summer's day on nature trails through the local woods, he gave me permission to go home. That was on the Thursday morning, and I left the *dojo* before training on the pretext of getting a ticket, I rang several hours later to say I would be leaving first thing Friday morning and would be back the following week. In reality, of course, I had booked my ticket months before. So too had Tom and Hiro. I was about to head off to the UK for a week with my two best friends. Like the Christmas before, I was nervous about escaping, but again I needed the break and it came at just the right time. My OCD had worsened as the summer built up and I could feel my grasp on reality fading. As I boarded the plane, my bruises mostly healed, I knew I would come back in a week's time to a much healthier lifestyle.

* * *

I returned in time for the All-Japan Championships. This year it was taking place in Tokyo, and international JKS affiliates had been invited to join the competition. It was basically a mini world championships. About thirty-five teams from around the world, including the UK and Irish teams, attended the technical seminar beforehand. It was great to see some of my old friends. For many competitors it was a rare chance to train at the Mecca of karate, to be part of a major international event and to experience Japanese, and therefore karate culture, first hand. Instructor training at the *hombu* was cancelled for a week as we prepared, putting the final touches to this large event. It was hot, I was busy and we all had the pressure of the championships looming in the not-too-distant future, but to my surprise I was relaxed and enjoying the moment. Several close friends were staying in Ikebukuro, so for the week I cancelled my classes and spent as much time as possible with them. My *sempai* were fine with my absence. They had told me I was to look after the foreign competitors, which I was doing. My phone number had been given out to every *gaijin* in a 200-mile radius and it was ringing non-stop, but on the whole the week was burden-free. Several of the countries took it upon themselves to think of me as their lackey, so any problems during their stay were taken out on me. Fortunately, this only lasted until the day of the technical seminar, when they found out I was one of the instructors and I took great delight in running rings around them during training.

In the evenings I met up with the UK and Irish teams. I had introduced them to Tengu and they had taken up permanent residence there. I had all my friends around me, but at the same time I was in Japan, translating for them all and helping them. These people knew me before Japan and they knew what the instructors' course was all about. They were world-standard *karate-ka* and to earn their respect in the way that I did meant a lot.

The first day of the competition was slightly more frantic than the week before. Competitors were missing their calls and I was given the task of running all over the massive arena to find them. I was also supposed to compete. My initial fights were good and I won decisively, but in the third round I came up against a Teikyo student and lost, partly because I was having to deal with an administrative problem flagged up by a member of the Indian team literally as I was being called up to fight. As I walked onto the mat, I promised him I would find the tea to go with his free lunch as soon as I had finished competing. I wasn't in the moment and so I lost – not badly, but still I lost. However, I had fought well. Takahashi Sempai had seen me and as I walk passed him moments later, he gave me a nod.

The following day was much better. People had realized that the numbers on their back closely resembled the numbers that were being called out, so often managed to find their way to the correct mat at the correct time. The second day was given over to *kata* and the finals. Without the constant barrage of complaints and demands I could prepare myself. My first opponent was the chief instructor of Canada. Yamamoto Sensei, a graduate of the instructors' course maybe fifteen years earlier. He was a talented *karate-ka* and, as he was such a senior instructor, I was unsure why he had decided to compete. I beat him and continued to win my rounds, including several Teikyo students, until the finals. I had made it to the best eight. I rested in the afternoon and prepared myself for the finals, feeling surprisingly relaxed. I had competed at world level before and it was always nerve-racking. The first time, at the 1993 JKS World Championships in South Africa, I threw up all the way to the venue. Now I felt at ease.

I came fourth, which wasn't bad. I thought I was better than the Teikyo student who came third and the UK and Irish teams were talking about racist judges not allowing a *gaijin* to win a medal in the All-Japan Championships, but I didn't care. I had done well and that was all that mattered, not only to my *sempai*, but also to me. Sueki won the *kumite*, beating Takahashi Sempai in the final. It was a great climax to an impressive weekend's competition and I was over the moon for him, if not a little concerned about the consequences of him beating our *sempai* in front of the whole JKS. However, Sueki was the golden boy. Earlier in the summer he had won the World Games in Malaysia. These games were multi-style, international events and the sparring categories were divided into weight divisions. At 70 kg he was the best fighter in the world, so to beat Takahashi Sempai in a competition was not surprising, apparently. Everyone expected him to win. Whilst Takahashi Sempai helped organize the championships and Koyama Sempai (who had come over with the French team) and I translated and ran about after lost packed lunches, Sueki was left to prepare and get in the zone. It paid off and he fought like a demon.

After the championships we threw a massive party with the UK, Irish, Swiss and Canadian teams. I had been cut loose by the Japanese and had all evening to myself. The Irish set about telling me that every Celt is in search of the perfect party – the perfect *craic* – and it turned out to be just that. Competition success, being surrounded by familiar faces, spending the evening at an expensive *izakaya* and putting it all down to expenses: perfect. I remembered meeting Richard Amos the first time I was in Japan. Ishii Sensei had taken us to the JKS *hombu dojo*. Richard was *kenshusei* at the time and I had a quick chat with him before the instructors' course training started. I then met him again in 1993 at the World Championships in South Africa where he fought wonderfully and came third. I remember thinking how incredibly good at everything he was.

I wasn't comparing my karate to his. He had major competition success in his career, far more than I could dream of. However, what had so impressed me about Richard was the communication and connection with Japanese instructors, the confidence of living in Japan. My friends could now see that in me. I was even told that my karate had changed. It wasn't better than before, just different. My old *sempai* from the UK said that my karate now had a quality about it that they couldn't quite define but were only used to seeing in Japanese instructors. They talked about my fluidity, my relaxed movement – I found it hard to grasp what they meant. Whatever had changed, I was happy and comfortable within myself and that almost seemed surreal. I had become so used to feeling lost, unhappy and alone. This was different. Halfway through the party, a member from the UK team stuck her chopsticks vertically into her bowl of rice.

'For Christ's sake,' I said, 'Get those chopsticks out of the rice... that represents *death*!'

I said it without thinking, as if it were the most natural response in the world. My friend complied immediately and only now, long afterwards, can I see how native I had become.

* * *

At the end of August I was asked to climb Mt Fuji. In Japan the mountain is referred to as Fuji-san and is paid deity-like reverence – and so it should! I had been told by people that I must ski in Nakano, drink sake in Hokkaido, taste fish eyes from Okinawa and poison myself with pufferfish in Tokyo. Every one of them was a disappointment, but the beauty of Fuji-san is undeniable. Climbing it, however, is another story. They say in Japan that a wise man climbs Fuji-san once and a fool climbs it twice. Terry McNab was going to climb it for the fourth time. He was a friend who occasionally took me to lap-dancing bars when the Swiss bank he worked for paid him a ridiculously high bonus. He asked me to climb it with him and I couldn't say no. Seven of us set off one Saturday evening from Tokyo and arrived at a delicate little *ryokan* in the foothills of Fuji-san. We stayed the night and were up at dawn ready for the climb, regretting the several cans of Kirin beer we had drunk the night before. After breakfast we took the train to halfway up the mountain. No, we didn't cheat – everyone, apparently, gets the train and starts from halfway up. We then faced a five-, maybe six-hour climb to the top.

We began confidently. The gradient was gentle. I was assured that the many elderly ramblers who were making their way back down were not giving up but had climbed throughout the night, so they could watch the sunrise from the top of the mountain. Actually they were looking at us strangely. It turned out that to climb the mountain during the day was slightly odd. Why climb all the way up, just to come down? Surely you should be going up to do something and, as I found out, watching the sunrise was the only thing to do up there. With the mantra of 'We are climbing it because it is there', we pushed on. I rapidly discovered that the gentle slopes gave way to massive, steep and dangerously loose cliff faces that had to be negotiated on all fours. I have no idea how the elderly ramblers got up the mountain, and in the dark. My party were insisting they were just a few boulders, but I know a cliff face when I see one. I told them, in a rather high voice, that I had a degree in geography. Fortunately, after the cliff-like boulders were behind us, the mountain turned barren and bleak, the only feature being the dirt path zig-zagging upwards. It was steep, but no worse than the mountain I had climbed with Teikyo University the year before, and I was fitter and stronger. Nothing could stop me, except the altitude. As we climbed, our pack of seven began to thin out. Apart from me, the gang were all businessmen, expats who spent their days in suits behind a desk. As I expected, these people were taking their time, but I decided to keep up with Terry. He was the exception in the current crowd: fit, athletic and in his mid-thirties. He practised kung-fu to keep slim, although I suspected it was to impress the dancing girls at One-Eyed Jack's.

As the altitude increased my legs became decidedly heavier, but I couldn't quite understand why. I knew what my body was capable of, and what I was feeling compared to what I had done didn't tally. It was the strangest of feelings as I knew I could easily do this, but every ounce of my body was telling me a different story.

I carried on. Every couple of hundred metres there was a station. Ten stations in all, some with simple shops, others with places to sleep, I now understood how the old ramblers had made it to the top in the dark: they had climbed the hard part in the day, arrived at a station with a bed and then slept until just before dawn, giving themselves enough time to make it to the top to see the precious sunrise. Perfect Japanese logic: take the easy option and pretend you have do it the hard way!

At the first station I stopped Terry and quickly swallowed a bar of chocolate and a bottle of water. It barely helped; my blood sugar level was still frighteningly low. I stopped at the next station, then the next… I must have gone through six or seven bars at six or seven stations, but still I was feeling drained, and no matter how much chocolate I rammed down, the feeling of total exhaustion never left. Terry and I reached the summit in just over three and a half hours, fast by anyone's standards. I immediately collapsed and slept for nearly an hour, then woke with my heart pounding. Despite sleeping for that amount of time my resting heart rate was about a hundred. It was normally forty-five.

After a further hour the stragglers had made it to the top, rested and taken in the view. We decided to make our way down. I was determined to take it easy, but as I descended I began to feel rejuvenated. After thirty minutes my clothes were drenched in sweat, but I felt great. I couldn't understand why. As we waited for the others I explained my lethargy to Terry.

'Oh, yeah, that's altitude sickness,' he clarified.

Looking back, this was quite dangerous. After all the training I have done in my life, I still think climbing Mt Fuji was the most extreme physical task I have endured, but because I was so used to ignoring what my body was saying to me, I fought on and continued up the mountain. I don't know if I put myself in danger climbing Fuji-san at the speed I did, but I do know that if I had taken my time, I wouldn't have felt like throwing up throughout the entire ascent and that my heart wouldn't have been pounding to get out of my chest even after an hour's sleep. Furthermore, the top of Fuji-san was so disappointing. I could see why the old dears were looking at us oddly as we made our way up in the light. At the top there was nothing apart from several vending machines. After my sleep, whilst waiting for the rest of our group, I walked around the crater but found nothing of interest. Clouds covered the view of the ground, so looking down at them from above, rather than looking up from below, amused me for several seconds, but once I remembered that the same effect can be achieved by sitting in a plane, it lost its appeal. I then thought about how the vending machines were filled. There was certainly no road to the top, so I suspected young Coco-Cola trainees were given the dreaded task. All in all, however, these two fascinating thoughts hardly made the physical effort worthwhile.

Once everyone had regrouped we moved on to a natural spring, the local *onsen,* and soaked ourselves in heated water courtesy of Fuji-san, still an active volcano. We then made our way to the local *izakaya* and soaked ourselves in artificially chilled beer. It was a great day. The summit was barren and lifeless, grey and littered with Coke cans, but the sense of achievement made up for any disappointing aspects of the experience. Looking at Fuji-san from afar, I never get over the size and perfection of the wonderfully shaped volcano, but to have climbed it was something else.

I returned to the *dojo* the following day. Sueki knew what I had been planning to do and was eager to find out if I had made it to the top. I told him the good news and he must have then immediately passed on the information. Takahashi Sempai came out of the instructors' changing room, looking rather surprised.

'Did you climb Fuji-san?'

I gave him a proud '*osu'*.

He came slightly closer and said, 'I've never climbed Fuji-san.'

He never said well done, or mentioned it again. Maybe a couple of months earlier I would have seen it as a way of getting one over on him, but the situation had changed. Climbing Mount Fuji was something that I had wanted to do and no matter how hard, I had been determined to do it well. Maybe the instructors' course was the same after all.

Chapter Ten:

Tough Housewife Does Christmas

Hiro and Tom are sitting at the table getting drunk as they watch me inch around the kitchen. I have just scurried home from my cleaning job at the *hombu dojo*, bought groceries and drink and now have to start the mammoth job of preparing and cooking a three-course dinner for three people in a three-foot-long kitchen.

After an hour the sake has kicked in and, combined with hunger, my two abusive husbands are complaining that it is taking too long. I tried to dissuade them from ordering Christmas turkey pizza from our local Domino's. I promise the homemade vegetable soup, followed by roast turkey and all the trimmings, plus traditional Christmas pudding to finish, will be their best Christmas dinner ever. Hiro points out that this will be his first Christmas dinner ever and they fall back into their drunken demands for pizza. If they weren't laughing so hard I would be tempted to take a kitchen knife to them.

After three hours all the food has been prepped and is well on the way to being cooked. I join the drunken party of two. Tom has been out and bought snacks to soak up the alcohol and 'put them on' to the main event and I secretly toast my mum for all the hard work she must have put in to the twenty-eight Christmas dinners she has cooked me over the years.

Eventually, after four hours of cooking and several large cartons of warm sake masquerading as mulled wine, we start. A certain calm descends on the table. For what seems like the entire day, Hiro and Tom have sat watching me cook and predicted the worst. This wasn't helped by the fact that the stuffing my mum had sent over didn't cook at all in the bread-sized 'oven'. As I pulled the soggy, cold mixture from the lukewarm appliance, every doubt in my onlookers' minds was confirmed. They were not expecting much. In unison, as if in some death pact, they tasted the soup. Triumph. Success. Clean, empty plates and bowls. The JKS has stopped me from going home for Christmas, but they can't stop me from bringing a bit of Christmas to Japan.

I had checked the price of flights back to the UK for Christmas in November, and had been promised that they would not increase until perhaps the second week of December, so I decided to wait and see what the schedule would be. When would the *dojo* finish for the year? When could I get away? I didn't want to risk anything like the previous Christmas. Besides, Christmas Day fell on the Tuesday, so they would definitely finish Friday 21 December. I could leave again on the Saturday and be home in time for my birthday. It was a perfect plan, but I still waited until the schedule was up on the whiteboard at the *dojo* on the first of the month.

I was the toughest housewife in Japan. Every year we had to clean the *hombu* from top to bottom: *O-soji* – the honourable clean! The previous year we had spent most of the last week that the *dojo* was open, cleaning. Instead of instructor training, we had mopped, polished and basically kept out of *sempai*'s sight. It was like their Christmas present to us – a whole extra week without being beaten up. That had always been the case and, as far as I was aware, would always be the case. To my horror, the end of 2001 would be a little different.

On 1 December I picked up ¥80,000 from the bank. My plan was to go straight from the *dojo* to the travel agent and buy my ticket home. I walked in just as Takahashi Sempai was finishing writing up the schedule. Not wanting to appear too interested,

I fiddled about with the flask of cold tea that was kept just under the whiteboard. It was my daily job to keep it topped up and it gave me an excuse to linger. As predicted, the last day of training was Friday 21 December. However, *O-soji* was scheduled for the following Monday and Tuesday. In their world just another start of the week. In my world, Christmas Eve and Christmas Day. We wouldn't have the week of light training and cleaning duties that had taken place, apparently, since the beginning of the course. Instead we would have an extra two days added on to our year, just to clean.

My brain went into hyper-drive, exploring all possible responses to this unexpected occurrence and then analyzing and gauging the fallout from such actions. (I did this in no more than five seconds: a *sempai* would be back in the changing room any moment and if he found me staring at the schedule with a tear in my eye he would put two and two together and find reason to beat me up). The conclusion was that I couldn't risk doing the same thing two years running. I was so close to the end of this thing that it would be stupid to jeopardize my future. I would have to stay.

As Christmas approached, my support team back home went into overdrive. Parcels arrived every day. One would be filled with presents, all perfectly wrapped for Christmas morning. The next would be filled with every Christmas delicacy known to man. I cried every time they arrived. Tom had also decided to stay in Japan for Christmas. Navo didn't have *gaijin* holidays, so every 25 December foreigners from every country in the world would turn up to work and have to ask disgruntled *sararimen* and dull office ladies to conjugate the verb 'to be', when the whole time inside their heads they were screaming, '*Do you not know it's fucking Christmas Day?*'

Luckily, although he was working Christmas Eve and Boxing Day, Tom had Christmas Day off. Hiro was also off for Christmas Day, so we decided that we would meet at Hiro's and have a traditional lunch together. I was desperate for a bit of home: the

163

holidays had always been a happy time for my family and it was tearing me up to not be able to spend it with them, so I browbeat my friends into submission. I had to spend the day with people I cared for. They weren't in the same squalid situation I was in, so it took the offer of a three-course meal to entice them.

The holiday season was the best I could have hoped for. Christmas Eve I had arranged to go for a drink with Mark, a French/Moroccan guy who had come over with the French team for the International All-Japan Championships that summer and never left. He had dreams to join the instructors' course, so he was at the *dojo* every day. Despite my natural aversion to the French, we had become friends, although he was very observant of the *sempai/kohai* hierarchy so going out for a drink with him wasn't really a chance for me to escape my surroundings. But it was Christmas Eve, a night when restaurants and love hotels were filled with couples. Tom was out patronizing both types of establishment with Kaori. Hiro was with his fiancé, who had spent all day preparing a romantic supper. I didn't want to be left alone and neither did Mark.

We went to a *gaijin* bar somewhere in Shinjuku. Within minutes, two young Japanese girls sidled over and, with a quick 'hello', snuggled up to us. The one sitting next to me spoke perfect English. The one sitting next to Mark didn't. Mark spoke perfect English, French and Arabic but not, as yet, Japanese, so between my new friend and I, we translated and interpreted. (The Japanese believe that if you have a relationship on Christmas Eve, you will have a relationship all year. It is like our Valentine's Day, although the Japanese have their own version of that too – on Valentine's Day men give women presents and on White Day, exactly a month later, women give men presents. Christmas Eve is more important and it is imperative that you have a date.) And then, as if some alarm bell had gone off in their heads, our girls announced it was time for the last train – it wasn't, it was barely 11 pm, but I wasn't going to argue. We walked to the station. At the time

Mark was living at Teikyo University (they often had spare rooms in their dormitories and Yumoto Sensei had kindly put him up). Mark couldn't take his girl back to the dorm, so I quickly gave him instructions on where to find a love hotel, and wished him luck. He looked slightly puzzled, but excited. I told his girl to look after him. 'What am I supposed to do? He can't speak Japanese!' I heard Mark's girl whisper as we walked away.

'*Shou ga nai...* It's Christmas!' mine replied.

A day later I arrived at the *dojo* to find it empty. I also found a note from Sueki telling me that he had had to go somewhere with Takahashi Sempai and that he was really sorry, he would be leaving the remainder of the cleaning for me. Poetic justice for the year before, I thought, but it didn't bother me. I cleaned the windows inside and out, gave the floor a good scrubbing and then I was free to go home. The time difference was such that it was the perfect time to call my family to wish everyone a happy Christmas. Like some multinational corporate conference call, I spoke to my whole family as I opened each present. It took me almost an hour to work through the piles of packages. My apartment was floor to ceiling in Christmas wrapping paper and although I was alone, I could convince myself that we were in the same room. Happiness! Although there were a few tears when I hung up, I really felt we had been together. From there I went directly to the supermarket, bought the remaining vital supplies and headed to Hiro's.

The meal was a triumph. I had brought a pre-cooked turkey and managed to cook all the vegetables just like my mum did. The stuffing was a disaster, but in one of the packages I had opened from my family I found a very large Christmas pudding. I had brought cream, whipped it up and by dessert, the stuffing was a distant memory. We finished all three courses and at the end of the evening Tom and I poured ourselves out of Hiro's apartment and staggered back to mine singing carols. I think we may have had a few beers as well. Tom had already planned to stay on my spare futon, so it was late by the time we passed out, but I didn't care. I was on holiday. No more *dojo* for ten days. I was free to enjoy my Christmas holiday.

And I did! I had cancelled my English lessons for the time I was away. Most students didn't want lessons anyway and the ones that did were the real pains in the arse. I could do without their money for a week or so. From Boxing Day to New Year I met friends for lunch, went to the cinema and watched videos. I even did a bit of shopping for myself. I pottered about for a whole week without realizing how good I had become at doing nothing in particular, and by the time New Year's Eve was approaching, I was practically an expert. Of course, it was still lonely, foreign and very different from being at home with my family, but compared to the stress I faced on a normal daily basis, this was heaven.

* * *

When Sueki found out that I had nothing planned for New Year he kindly invited me to his family home for the holiday. It was a great honour, like being invited for Christmas lunch to a family you don't really know, except I would be staying with them for three days. I really looked forward to it and it was arranged that I would meet Sueki at Omiya Station, about one hour north of Tokyo, at 7 am on New Year's Day. I had also planned to go out with Tom on New Year's Eve in Ebisu and that twelve-hour period from 9 pm at night to 9 am in the morning perfectly represented how I had split myself in two whilst in Japan. The years of walking to the *dojo* pretending that it wasn't going to be that bad, whilst knowing it would be; the years living in one of the most extreme forms of Japanese society then returning home and teaching English and earning a living by being a caricature of an English gent; the years of socializing one night with my *gaijin* friends in Roppongi, then the following night with my *sempai* in some exclusive Japanese-only hostess bar. The way that my life had been partitioned and the more I lived there, the smaller my English part became. All these things were highlighted by New Year 2002.

New Year's Eve, as long as you are surrounded by western-ers, is much the same anywhere. The backdrop may be different, the drinks may have exotic names, but a drunken American is a drunken American throughout the world. Ebisu was no different. We spent the night in What The Dickens, an English-themed bar were I could buy cider, my tipple of choice, for about £6 per pint. We had already lined our stomachs with cheap Japanese beer at the local *izakaya*, so after three pints of cider I no longer worried about the exorbitant prices. Besides, What The Dickens was full of hot Japanese girls. Unlike the meat markets of Roppongi, the girls here were a better class of I-am-desperate-to-marry-a-foreigner, and the I-have-to-come-to-Japan-to-lose-my-virginity *gaijin* were far less geeky than their Roppongi counterparts. I was having a great time and vaguely remember making fun of George W. Bush to an American girl, shamelessly using Jay Leno jokes I had seen on TV, hoping that she was so far from home she hadn't heard them. I was either right or she appreciated the effort as we got on rather well. Tom, being Tom, did well too. He constantly amazed me how he could pull, even in the most inhospitable of climates. For him, What The Dickens may as well have been heaven as he social-butterflied his way around the room.

Unfortunately, things degenerated and the night ended in an argument. It was probably my fault. I am sure it was over a girl. I had moved on from the American girl – or she had moved on from me – and I found myself next to the rather beautiful Japanese girl who Tom had in his sights. Being able to speak fluent Japanese, I launched into a familiar pantomime of '*Gaijin*'s first steps on planet Japan'. She found it amusing, but Tom wasn't so impressed, and rightly so. Things were said that involved 'get your own girl', 'butt out' and 'fuck off'. I was on the receiving end of most of them.

In hindsight, this episode may have been the proverbial straw that broke the camel's back of our friendship. Although Tom had only been in Japan for a little over a year, I had unwittingly dragged him into my own personal hell. A particular bugbear of his was that I insisted we go out and party every Friday night, which inevitably ended up with us becoming hideously drunk. Although we both taught English early on a Saturday morning, I didn't care in the slightest, and, looking back, I can see that I may have been a functioning alcoholic. I know Tom now understands my need to escape from my reality but at the time it was less obvious. Coupled with my mood swings, I am surprised the blow up didn't happen sooner. Either way, for the rest of the time I was in Japan, Tom and I never quite saw eye to eye, although all is good now.

I crawled back to my hole on the first train of the day. Alone, drunk yet already hungover, I had managed to alienate one of my closest friends, a pillar I had clung to ever since his arrival in Japan. I could argue with myself whether I was justified or not. I was drunk, so was he; I was just having a laugh with the girl, so was he; I was single, he wasn't... but it made little difference. I had lost one of my last remaining contacts with the western community of Tokyo.

I headed to Omiya after a quick shower and a dose of sobering medication, one of the ubiquitous magical power drinks sold to energize the Tokyo work force. I had to report for 7 am and I could just make it. The journey seemed to take forever and to my befuddled mind it felt as if I were leaving behind the last remnants of foreignness. I was about to spend three days immersed in Japanese culture at such a special time of year that few outsiders would ever dream of the possibility, but I felt perfectly at home with it. Perhaps the argument with Tom had finally pushed me over the edge. Staggering into the sunlight at Omiya, I called Sueki to come and collect me.

The bastard was still asleep!

'Uh, uh... Nani?' came the reply.

'I'm here, waiting for you!' I felt like I had covered the entire length of Japan and still made it on time for him to pick me up. We were travelling north up to the mountains to Sueki's father's family home, and everyone was supposed to be up, to witness the first sunrise of the New Year. Not Sueki – he was still sleeping like a teenager and his snappy reply was only slightly overshadowed by my even more irritable demand that he get out of bed and get his arse down to the station to collect me. He finally arrived and drove me back to the family home. It was my first visit and I had only previously met his dad. To my horror I found myself still slurring my words as I was introduced to his mum and sister. The *Genki-juice* I had taken obviously hadn't worked, so I fought frantically against my body, trying to prevent it from acting like some drunken, foreign bum. I was facing a losing battle and when I discovered that we wouldn't be going to the mountains for another hour or two, suggested it might be a good idea if I had some sleep. Sueki's mum was very sweet – obviously his brutality wasn't a family trait – and showed me to the spare room, made up a futon, put the heater on and left me with some water. I hopped into bed and fell asleep before I could make more of a fool of myself.

When I woke up three hours later and stumbled downstairs the family were waiting for me. Sueki greeted me with a 'Shall we go?' and before I could wipe the sleep from my eyes, we were in the car and off. They all seemed very kind. This was their Christmas Day and I remember thinking that if I had brought home some drunken fool on such a special day and forced my family to look after him, I doubt my parents would have been so accommodating. But one should never underestimate the draw of a *gaijin* and before long we were into the Japanese-meet- *gaijin* -for-the-first-time conversation. I answered the usual can you use chopsticks/oh your Japanese is good/do you eat sushi questions with ease and by the time we were leaving behind the pollution of the Tokyo metropolis, the Sueki family seemed at ease with the cuckoo sitting in their nest.

The journey took over three hours and I would love to be able to say where we travelled to, but like some Miyazaki animation, the

Genki. This is used all the time to mean full of life, lively, well – anything positive in a physical way.

hero of this story was completely clueless as to either where he was or what he was doing. We arrived at Sueki's paternal grandparents' house. It was huge, some sort of castle on the side of a mountain with a labyrinth of corridors and rooms. I was shown my bedroom and then Sueki quickly brought me into the main dining room. Sueki's sister and mother were already in the kitchen with a number of other women of various ages and there they would remain for the entire two days of our stay. I was never introduced to any of the women, who were made up of various generations of the Sueki family. Obviously the feminist revolution hadn't made it this far east yet. A similar number of generations on the male side sat around a very large table and I was introduced as Sueki's *doki*, Scott from England. The news was received by a unanimous '*sugoi*' but I was unsure what they were impressed with. The fact I was *kenshusei*? The fact I was English? Maybe it was my name that was the clincher? Either way, I must have been a hit with the group and was handed a beer. A woman with X-ray vision was given the task of replacing each of the men's beer cans just before the last mouthful was consumed. Meanwhile, the rest of the hired help were busying themselves in the kitchen. Maybe X-ray woman could also see into stomachs, as just as we were about to mention we were hungry, a fresh new plate of food was brought in; each different from the last and increasingly tastier as they went along. The party finished at about midnight, and considering I had been going for two days without a full night's sleep, I felt remarkably well. In spite of this, my futon was a welcome relief.

We were woken at dawn for some hunting. I was given fluorescent overalls and boots and we gathered at the gate of the house. Sueki's father, Mr Sueki, had grown up in the area and brought along three of his high-school friends. One was his cousin, who was also called Sueki – there were far too many Suekis around for me

---

Sugoi. Next to genki, sugoi is the most-used word in the Japanese language. (I can't believe I have got this far in the book without using them both.) Sugoi means terrific, great, brilliant – anything positive in a non-physical sense.

to keep track of. I ended up calling my Sueki, Yasu. Of course I knew that Yasu was Sueki's given name, but I had never called him by it, just like he never called me Langley. Calling him Yasu seemed strange, but it went with the slower pace of life here. He didn't bat an eyelid, but we both knew that once we returned to Tokyo, it would be back to Sueki.

The hunting party set off; the three high-school friends, Mr Sueki, Yasu and me. The three friends were inquisitive about the *gaijin*, asking Mr Sueki about me even as I stood right next to them. Mr Sueki did point out that I spoke perfect Japanese, but they preferred to keep a perceived safe, if not actual physical distance, by going through a mediator – I just hoped they didn't think I had come along to be hunted rather than to hunt. They had the look of tough country men. Having probably never seen a *gaijin* in the flesh before, it was easy to imagine them believing I wasn't human, just a fast target for their amusement. After all, I had just spent the last eighteen months being a rather slow target for my s *empai*. Thankfully, all turned out well. We went to the local woods and shot pigeons. Yasu could barely handle his shotgun and scared the birds away rather than shooting them, so I think they were reluctant to let the *gaijin* have a go. However, after a few hours of watching patiently, they handed me a gun. I used both barrels and bagged two birds. I said thank you for the loan of the gun and handed it back to Mr Sueki (the cousin). Modesty is always the best option in this type of situation. They had never bothered to ask me if I had shot before and I never bothered to tell them. However, my pair was on par with the two birds each of the rest of the group had bagged over the last couple of hours.

The Japanese can be so fickle. Like many other occasions during my time in Japan, one incident or event could completely change the views that people have of you. The shooting instantly made me one of them and the pats on the back and direct conversation ensued. We all followed high-school Friend No.1 back to a hut on the outskirts of the forest. By this time it was mid-morning and along with the ten birds, we crammed ourselves into this little potting shed. It had a dirt floor and a fire in the centre. It was quickly lit, we all sat around it, getting warm after a morning in bitterly cold weather. Friend No.1 disappeared and then reappeared with beer and sake. Everyone was handed a drink and we toasted a successful morning. The last thing I had the night before was a final beer to toast the New Year, the first thing I was having this morning was a beer to toast the hunt... I liked the Sueki family.

After a while Friend No. 2 returned with all the pigeons plucked, cleaned and skewered. They were placed on the fire and Friend No. 2 basted them with a sauce that he magically conjured from his pocket. Ten minutes later we were all helping ourselves to the pigeons we had just killed. It did make me feel a whole lot better about killing the birds – at least we were eating them.

The morning whizzed by. Various nibbles and vegetables were also brought out to go with the birds, and considering I was cold, tired and surrounded by complete strangers, I was made to feel welcome and included in the conversation. At about 2 pm, when we were all starting to feel the effects of the alcohol, Friend No.1 decided that we were all hungry again, left the shed and about two minutes later I heard several shots in the distance. He couldn't have, I thought: surely he has gone to order pizza or something. But he returned with four birds, quickly plucked and prepped them and before I knew it, friend No. 2 had his sauce out again and was basting away. Apart from the occasional piece of lead shot between the teeth, they were tasty. Not quite roast turkey, but delicious, basic food that I am sure I could have only experienced there and then.

That evening we sat around the large dining table again. We talked about the day and Mr Sueki took some pride in telling the rest of the men about my shooting skills. I felt at home with these people and I remember thanking Yasu at the end of the night. It had been a hard Christmas. Hiro and Tom had helped me get through Christmas Day, but that was all it was, a way of getting through it. Yasu, however, helped me enjoy New Year. With the state of mind that I was in before I travelled to Omiya, that was no easy feat.

Before we left, Grandfather Sueki decided he wanted to give me a present. He sent his wife scurrying and several minutes later she came back with a box. He fished inside and brought out three small, ancient-looking leather bags, which he told me to open. Inside the first was an antique pipe.

'It is an old Samurai pipe,' he explained. I didn't know what to say. I opened the next and found a delicate fob watch.

'Same. Samurai,' he added.

Speechless, I think I managed to say, '*Hai, wakarimashita*' ('Yes, I understand'). I opened the third and found a *tsuba*, an ancient samurai sword hand guard. Decorated with a carving of a dragon, it was old and dirty, but heavy and authentic with an amazing, intricate design. I wouldn't know what to say in English, never mind Japanese, and 'thank you very much' just sounded so feeble, but that is what I eventually came up with. I think I managed a 'you are very kind' as well, but it all paled into insignificance to what he had given me. He said it was nothing and told me to take care: not of the things he had given me, but to take care of myself. Those two days were the only time I met Grandfather Sueki and the extended Sueki family, but what kindness! I hadn't been able to make it back to my home for the holidays, but at least I had made it to a home and that was enough for now.

We arrived back to Yasu's family home late on 3 January. Mr Sueki made us watch the well-worn World Karate Federation tape of Yasu winning the world championships. There was obvious pride in his father's face. After the viewing, Mr Sueki asked me to come and see the family shrine. Most Japanese houses would have a Shinto shrine in one of their rooms where they would pray for good fortune. Shintoism, the native religion of Japan, is simply a set of ideas with a variety of gods rather than a dogmatic religion. The joke is that the Japanese are born into Shintoism (the local priest is usually asked to bless newborns), marry Christian (the Japanese love the romantic imagery of church weddings) and die Buddhist (they will be cremated at the local Buddhist temple). The shrine wasn't different to other family shrines I had seen in other houses, but Mr Sueki explained that every time Yasu competed, Mr Sueki would pray that he wasn't injured. He never prayed for victory, just that he would be safe. Yasu had mentioned that his father was an avid fan and financial supporter of *Maui Thai* boxing. He had been to Thailand over thirty times to watch and support bouts. He may have done some training himself when he was young, but when I mentioned it to him, he sidestepped the issue and went immediately back to talking about his son. The pride was still there and although everyone knows that Maui Thai boxers are tough, Mr Sueki knew his son was tougher.

The night finished with a re-run of the final match between Sueki and a guy from eastern Europe. The guy came in with a beautiful reverse roundhouse kick, Yasu shifted out of the way and scored with the very same kick. Unbelievable! I trained with him everyday, but his timing and skill could still surprise me. It was quite understated. To deliver that sort of technique in the finals of a world championship was talent in the extreme. Like his father, I was very proud of him too. As the rest of the family watched the TV, Yasu told me that when he was young, he had seen the world championship final on video and had promised himself that one day he too would be there, competing and winning at that level – watching it now, he often couldn't believe he was looking at himself.

I remember clearly being seventeen years old and meeting Richard Amos at a training camp at York University. He was on the instructors' course in Tokyo and had come over to the UK with Teikyo University and Yumoto Sensei. He was an excellent fighter, better than any of the Teikyo students, spoke fluent Japanese and his karate was like no other westerner's I had ever seen. I had immediately wanted to do the same as him. Ten years later, I was here, doing what he did, speaking fluent Japanese and improving my karate. Sueki, however, was world champion, and because I was so used to feeling dejected I automatically deemed my own accomplishments as less significant. Maybe it was because I had been so well looked after, but at that moment I began to gain a little bit of self-confidence. I was so close to finishing this thing. If I did, I would become only the fifth westerner to complete the course in its fifty-five-year history. There are world champions every year in many different categories but there have only been a hundred graduates of the instructors' course, ever, less than two per year, and out of those one hundred, only four had been westerners. Perhaps if I got through the next few months, I could be the fifth. Surely that is something to be proud of?

Yasu woke me early the next morning to say goodbye. He was leaving for national team training camp. He didn't think it was important enough to mention it to me before he left, so after a quick 'see you later' he was gone. Perhaps he was in denial too; maybe he didn't want his holiday spoilt by thinking about having to go back to the *dojo*. I wandered downstairs and was greeted by a chorus of *'Ohayou Gozaimasu'* – a loud and headache inducing way of saying "good morning". My plan was to get washed and changed, say my *arigatos* and travel back to Tokyo, but Mr Sueki had different plans.

'We will leave in ten minutes,' he explained as I tucked into my eggs. There was a Maui Thai fight at the Tokyo Dome and we were going.

We arrived early lunchtime, parked up and wandered to one of the many restaurants for a spot of lunch. Every other person was stopping to say hello to Mr Sueki: it seemed that although he had no idea who most of them were this was a usual occurrence. These nameless people were mainly young, trying to get into the inner circle, but several older and important-looking men also stopped to say hello. Mr Sueki took his time with these guys and chatted about the fights that afternoon. To my amazement, he always introduced me. He explained who I was and the connection I had

175

with his son. They all knew Yasu and seemed genuinely interested in my story. I was the only *gaijin* I saw all day, which is a little unusual for the centre of Tokyo, and I knew nothing about Maui Thai, but yet again, Japanese hospitality always caught me out when I was most off guard.

After a delicious lunch and several beers with what must have been the 'inner' inner circle, we were shown our ringside seats and watched the fights. They were tough young guys, cracking shin against shin. All the time I was, thankfully, getting a running commentary from Mr Sueki, which was thoroughly enjoyable. Not long before I had had to switch off a world boxing championship on TV as I had been going through a particularly bad time at the *dojo*. Watching any more violence, even violence so far removed, was too much to handle. I loved a good boxing match, but found myself turning over to *Ally McBeal* instead. Now I was ringside as bone-crushing kicks were sunk in only metres away, but it all felt fine.

As the last fight ended it was time for me to leave. I bowed my deepest thank you to Mr Sueki and said I must make my way home. He seemed surprised. He expected me to return to Omiya, but as we only had a few more days before training resumed, I had to get back; besides my plan had always been to go home on the third. Maybe this was something else Yasu had failed to share with anyone else. Mr Sueki said he understood and handed me money for the taxi fare home. Again, the level of hospitality blindsided me. I hadn't spent a penny since arriving at the Sueki household, and it wasn't through lack of trying. Mr Sueki had just entertained me all day, as well as treating me to a great lunch. This was too much. I hoped I didn't insult him by refusing the money, but I replied with a firm 'NO' and apologized in true Japanese fashion: I left walking backwards, whilst bowing.

* * *

On 7 January I returned to the *dojo*. I was resolute. No more OCD.

I still got up at the same time, took the same trains and sat on the same seats, but this had become a tradition and not a manifestation of the disorder. Everything else was gone. I also never threw up before training again. It was a promise to myself that I would not allow them the satisfaction of making me so nervous that I started retching (the owner of the barber shop along the alley that I always used was also very happy not to see me running past the window, projectile vomit leading the way). I had four more months to go and I was going to make it.

Chapter Eleven:

Carpe Diem'd Out

I am surrounded by sixty of my closest friends... incredible, but true. On one table are the very finest of Navo students. On another table are the remaining Navo teachers I know, the ones who haven't left for home over the years. Another table is filled with my private English students. They have stuck with me through blood and bruises for all these years. Opposite them are the *hombu dojo* students. Some have only been members since I started the instructors' course and they are finding it hard that I am insisting they don't call me *sensei*. Others are from way back and are looking at me with pride. Sueki and Hirota, our new *Kohai*, are in there somewhere too. The rest is made up of people I just know. I don't know where from, I am simply glad they are here. In three days' time I will leave Japan for ever, and this is the perfect finish.

The night is coming to an end. Everyone is leaving. I am hugged and kissed by the very affectionate gaijin and drunken Japanese. Sueki is the last to go.

'Take care.' What else can I say? 'I will see you soon.'

It is a lie. I go to shake his hand, I don't want to be the overemotional foreigner, but as I do he lunges for me, delivering a fierce hug. I realize he is sobbing as he buries his head in my shoulder. Everyone else has gone except Hirota, and he makes himself scarce.

Through the deep intakes of breath, I hear, 'Don't go... why do you have to go?... Don't go.'

'I am sorry,' and I truly am. I don't want to leave my brother but I have to go. I say this to him, but again everything I say sounds cowardly and weak. I start to cry too. I hug him again and say I don't want to leave. I half-heartedly explain that I will always be a foreigner here and I need to start my life elsewhere. I can't do it here. He still asks me not to go. I take him outside. He is still crying and so am I. Finding Hirota, I wish him luck and let him take Sueki. Tom is patiently waiting to take me home.

Why, after all these years, is this the hardest part?

I returned to the dojo after Christmas, a rejuvenated man. It was cold, crisp weather, perfect for training. There was no competition looming, so the bloodbaths were put on hold. We knew that we would be graduating soon and Sueki still didn't know all the twenty-six *kata* of Shotokan karate. So, after *kangeiko* at the end of January, our training mainly consisted of basics, tube training and then the final part of the session was set aside for *kata* practice.

Perfect, the three things I could do as well as most of them, certainly Sueki anyway. I was becoming comfortable and relaxed in the *dojo*, as was Sueki: he no longer had to run to the toilet three times in the five minutes before training and we both seemed to fit as *sensei*. I became a little more confident. I started to ask questions of Takahashi Sempai during training about certain techniques or *kata*. At one point, when he was asking Sueki which *kata* he still did not know – somewhat redundantly, as Sueki didn't know which *kata* he didn't know – I asked for him to teach us *Jiin*. It is one of the twenty-six Shotokan *kata*, but is often overlooked, so much so that in two years of training we had never done it. I even explained this to Takahashi Sempai and he looked at me in

---

Kangeiko. Cold training. Starting on the last Monday of January many members of the dojo would meet at 7 am, jog around the streets and then return to train until 8 am. Continuing for a week, on the Sunday we would jog to the local Shinto shrine, pray for good luck and then return to the dojo for a party. It's a way of building dojo spirit.

horror. In the past I would have got a beating for reminding him of a certain inadequacy of the training, but this time I got a look of, 'Oh, Jesus', and we set about doing *Jiin*. I had finally been accepted.

As spring approached I started to think seriously about what I wanted to do after graduation. My *sempai* never asked directly – such a blatant show of emotion was still too much for them – but a subtle question here and an understated comment there meant that I knew they wanted to know exactly what I had planned and when I planned to do it. And they had a secret spy, Sueki. I was managing to evade all questions, though. The timing of the disclosure of my plans was very important: knowledge is power, and the less power my *sempai* had, the better. Since starting the course I had hoped that one day it would lead to me being able to move to Dublin and teach full time. My plan was that in the summer or autumn of 2002, I would leave Japan and move to Ireland, but there was still the problem of how exactly I was going to do that. Very few people knew me in Ireland and I had a feeling I was going to have problems with Ishii Sensei back in the UK.

Relations with Ishii Sensei and the JKS had become increasingly strained over the years. Politics play a huge part in karate. Great masters, who are perceived as being the bastions of humility, honour and truth, can often turn into egotistical monsters. It happens all the time, and due to personality clashes and certain alcohol-fuelled idiosyncrasies, Ishii Sensei was thrown out of the JKS. However, thanks to his close personal contact with Taguchi Sensei, he was now the European Chief Instructor of the Traditional Budo Karate Federation. It was an organization loitering around the edges of the JKS and Taguchi Sensei became the World Chief Instructor of both the JKS and the TBKF. It was the elephant in the room. Nothing could be said as Taguchi Sensei was the head of our group, and no *hombu dojo* instructor in their right mind would question Taguchi Sensei's authority. With this as the backdrop I started to make plans to return to Europe. Due to Ishii Sensei's influence, there were very few JKS affiliates in Europe. Most people thought that the TBKF was the new name for the Taguchi-Sensei-headed group after we had lost a court battle for the use of the name *JKA* in 1999. People also believed that Yumoto Sensei and all the *hombu dojo* instructors were TBKF and that Ishii Sensei was the representative of the *hombu dojo* in Europe. This, of course, was not true and my returning and setting up the JKS in the UK might create a problem for Ishii Sensei. Ireland was a safer, more diplomatic option.

I began to hatch a plan. By February we only had a month or so before graduation. I needed to become known back home, and what better way to do that than through a teaching tour. I was also desperate for another holiday. Going home to teach alone would have been pointless: I would simply be some anonymous third dan. Some people vaguely knew me from a teaching trip I had taken with Yumoto Sensei the year before, but not enough. So I enrolled the help of Sueki, who was not only world champion, but was also Japanese. The western karate world is often inherently racist. If you are Japanese, you must be a great *sensei*. If you are western, you are often seen as another student. So if I brought Sueki, they would come along to train with him, see me, and hopefully appreciate that I was just as good. I broached the subject with Yumoto Sensei and he thought it was a splendid idea. The week after graduation we would go to the UK and Ireland for a ten-day teaching tour. All that lay in the way was graduating.

The day was scheduled for 16 March. Our trip home had been arranged, and the *sensei* knew my long-term plans. It was no longer possible for me to stay, as five years had not only drained

---

JKA. Originally all shotokan karate was controlled by a group called the Japan Karate Association. The founder, Nakayama Sensei, died in 1987 and Taguchi Sensei was made Chief Instructor. However, following disagreements with the administration director in 1989 the JKA split and two fractions were formed. Taguchi Sensei headed one fraction, and a ten-year legal battle followed for the right to use the name. Taguchi Sensei conceded in 1999 and we had to change our name to JKS.

me physically and emotionally, but also financially. I would have to go sooner rather than later, but I didn't just want to graduate and then run away. I wanted to stay for a bit, prove I could do it, and then go. Sueki had persistently asked what I was going to do and so a week before the graduation I told him my plan: I would leave mid-summer. I didn't realize he would go straight to our *sempai* and tell them.

Graduation day arrived. Everyone had turned up, including the old unknowns who were at our entrance exam, Matsumura Sensei eighth dan and Hashimoto Sensei eighth dan. They sat in the middle, flanked by Taguchi Sensei and Yumoto Sensei.

'*Seiritsu!*' The command to line up was given. Sueki moved to the centre of the *dojo* and I went to follow, but Yamada Sempai blocked my way and with a snigger told me to stand with them. I didn't understand. Why wasn't I lining up? Moments later Takahashi Sempai announced that we were here to witness the graduation of Sueki. I wasn't graduating. Sueki did his one *kata* and broke three wooden boards and that was it, he was now a *hombu dojo* instructor. I was still *shugyosei* and in shock.

We went to the local restaurant and had a celebratory meal. Still no one had explained anything to me, but after the initial toast, Takahashi Sempai sidled up. Perhaps he had been given the job of telling me the truth. He explained that Taguchi Sensei had decided that I needed an extra three months to bring my technique up to standard. Therefore, he explained, I would complete the course just before I returned home. It was at this point that it all fitted into place. It was their last way of showing me the difference, their last way of testing me, their last way of pushing me down just a little bit more. It worked. I was heartbroken. My expression must have betrayed my feelings because Takahashi Sempai filled my glass with beer, picked up his own and toasted me. In a whisper he congratulated me for finishing the course and I knew then that these next couple of months were a formality. I had finished and passed in all but name. I could wait three months for a certificate.

Shortly after Sueki and I travelled to the UK. We stayed at my parents' house for a day or two and then set out on our mammoth tour of the UK and Ireland. It was a huge success. People came from every major association to train with us and most of them were friendly and open. We both taught good lessons and the comments we received afterwards was positive. We had achieved what I had set out to do.

Of course there were times when some participants of the course completely dismissed me as just another translator, someone who was there simply to assist, but I quickly learnt that people often make judgements based on a whole host of criteria, not just what they see in front of them. At first these people upset me. I was a foreigner in Japan and then when I returned home I was still a foreigner. I think they baulked when they saw an English guy doing karate like the Japanese. Allegedly the Japanese have greater flexibility in their hips and ankles, due to the way they sit on the floor all the time as well as an indomitable fighting spirit inherited from their samurai ancestors. They naturally excel in martial arts due to historical factors, which infiltrate every part of their culture. Western *karate-ka* have been using these excuses for years to explain why they are not as good as the Japanese. I slightly spoiled those excuses, which is why some people didn't take to my karate. I also actively fought against these clichés and the merest mention of them would invoke a diatribe from me. The 'naturally flexible' excuse would cause me to explain that Yumoto Sensei couldn't do the splits until he was in the second year of university and only did so after his *sempai* forced him into the position. With the 'fighting spirit' argument, I would remind people that the Japanese actually lost the World War II. And when people presumed that Japan was the birthplace of martial arts, I would point out that every country had its own system, it was just that Japan didn't modernize and kept the feudal system going until the end of the nineteenth century, giving the martial ways time to develop into art forms (in the UK wrestling and boxing became sports and staff fighting transformed itself into Morris dancing!) A long article was written about us in the leading international karate magazine, calling us 'the next generation of karate *sensei*'. We went back to Japan a little more famous and a little more experienced. I had also met with people in Ireland and the foundations for me to move over and teach there full time were set. It was all looking good.

* * *

The next few months flew by. We had a new *kohai*. Hirota had come to us from the normal source, Teikyo University, where as captain he had been asked to enter the instructors' course. He was everything that I had come to expect from members of the Teikyo University squad. He was fast, aggressive, talented and waddled along the road, just like Yumoto Sensei, but unlike the others, Hirota was only twenty-two years old. He looked like a small boy and giggled a lot, but once he got going, he moved with the speed of Takahashi Sempai. It was great to train with him as I could really fight without the need to worry about being hit. I was his *sempai*, he wouldn't hit me, and like Kawada the year before, it was enjoyable to spar in a natural manner. The last two years of training had taught me something and I now had an outlet for the lessons I had learnt.

My days in Japan were numbered, and very soon we were into June. The weather was starting to warm up and I had to book my flight home... actually not quite home. I had kept a credit card, unused for my entire time in Japan. It was labelled: FOR USE IN EMERGENCY ONLY! This was an emergency. My plan was to fly back to the UK with a stopover in the USA. I would fly to Los Angles, spend a month travelling across America and then fly home from New York. I had friends in Austin, Philadelphia, Boston and New York and I was about to ask for a few favours, so booking my flight and a one-month unlimited Amtrak train pass was at the forefront of my mind. But I wasn't going to leave before I graduated. At the beginning of June I spoke to Yumoto Sensei and told him that I would have to leave sometime this summer. My financial situation back in the UK was getting worse and I had to return home and start earning money. I needed to know when I would graduate.

'When do you want to leave?' came the reply. I thought about it, and said the beginning of July.

'Umm...' he looked over at the calendar. There was a national technical seminar planned for the middle of June. He pointed to it marked on the calendar and said, 'Then!'

I would test on the seminar and leave at the beginning of July. That wasn't all, I would also take my *yondan* - 4 th degree black belt - at the seminar. This really took me by surprise: Sueki was only *sandan* and a long way from taking *yondan* as he only graded when he became *kenshusei*. I never thought they would grade me before him.

It all happened so quickly. Two weeks later I was standing in front of Taguchi Sensei. Two older gentlemen had just gone before me and taken seventh and eighth degree black belt. I was there to perform a few *kata* and fight Sueki. I did *Sochin* and *Bassai Dai*, the two *kata* that had got me on the course. Taguchi Sensei was pleased. I then had to fight Sueki. Taguchi Sensei asked me what unique quality I brought to my *kumite*. Maybe sweeping jaw block... I had used that successfully against Takahashi Sempai. Maybe adding projectile vomit to my *kiai*, that too had been effective. However, I opted for *Yokogeri Keage* – side snap kick. No one used that in *Jiyu-kumite*, but I found it worked. I always attacked from a forty-five-degree angle, really extended my hips, and the opponents never knew what was coming. Without explaining, I did it on Sueki and it worked perfectly. The test was short and sweet. No breaking of the boards, just, 'That's it, let's go to the pub.'

The Saturday ended with all the senior grades drunk in an *izakaya* around the corner from the *dojo*. Hirota was *osu* -ing and bowing his way from table to table and Sueki and I sat with senior grades from around the country. We were part of the team, and although regional heads of JKS Japan had always treated me well, on this occasion they seemed to do so with a greater amount of respect, although maybe that was my own interpretation. Unfortunately, by the end of the night no one had mentioned anything about my test. Had I passed? Was I still *Shugyosei*? Was I still *Sandan*? Or had I passed both tests? Maybe I would find out at the end of the technical seminar.

On Sunday we turned up bright and early. On this particular course there were about forty-five regional heads and club instructors from all over Japan. Everyone was *godan* – fifth degree black belt - and above, so most were well in to their forties and fifties. Training was never hard, compared to *kenshusei* training, so it didn't matter if we were hungover or not. Taguchi Sensei taught a brilliant course on the correct way to inhale and exhale, teaching two breathing *kata* that he had learnt from a martial arts master in China. This is why I had come to Japan. Two weeks before leaving and I had found what I was looking for. Still, by the end of the course nothing had been mentioned about my test and I left the *dojo* late on Sunday evening without a clue. I had two weeks left. What was I supposed to do, go over to Taguchi Sensei's office and say, 'So Sensei, what's the story?'

I put it out of my mind, determined to enjoy my last fortnight. My English lessons were winding down. My friends had organized a farewell party on Sunday 30 June and I would be leaving on Wednesday 3 July, exactly five years to the day that I had moved to Japan. It seemed fitting. I had met an Englishwoman, Samantha, when I had flown over to the UK with Sueki several months earlier. We had got drunk together on the plane, exchanged email addresses and had become friends very quickly. She was the driving force behind my party and I found that all of a sudden I was in a great place, as the Americans like to call it. So why was I leaving? Realistically, I still couldn't live and teach karate here professionally. It was time to go, but this new level of contentment made me realize how much I loved Japan. I saw myself as half Japanese. There was nowhere I couldn't go, no one I couldn't talk to and nothing I couldn't experience in all its idiosyncratic beauty. I was a Japanophile and proud of it.

A week before I left, Samantha took me to a *Kyodo dojo*, the elaborate form of Japanese archery that has been turned into a *budo* – a martial art. She had friends at the *dojo* and had arranged for us both to have a go. Samantha – who could also speak very good Japanese – and I spent two hours having a lesson with a sixth degree black belt of *Kyodo*. As part of their regular training, black belts from the local area had come over to take part. Their training took a back seat as they all turned their attention to Samantha and I, helping and encouraging us. We were told that it normally took six months of training before the *sensei* would let a beginner shoot an arrow, but as I only had a week left, he would forgo this rule. Consequently, for an hour and a half, we were given a lesson on the correct way to walk, stand and hold the bow. We were then given a further twenty-minute lesson on how to correctly notch the arrow and pull it back. I couldn't imagine how much patience it must take to do solely this for six months. Maybe it was the extreme contrast to the *budo* lessons I had experienced over the last five years, but they seemed worlds apart. During the last ten minutes we were finally allowed to shoot ten arrows. It was much harder than I thought: the odd, tear-drop-shaped bow, designed to be fired on horseback, produced power if shot correctly and a limply responding arrow if shot incorrectly. However, by the fifth arrow I was in the zone. I heard the *sensei* talking to Samantha, who mentioned I was a *yondan* in karate. Was I? I still hadn't heard anything from Taguchi Sensei.

'*Yappari so ne...*' he replied, which roughly translates to, 'Yes it is plainly obvious, isn't it?' I was so very pleased with myself that the next two arrows were crap. I thought I had better make the last three arrows count – I still hadn't hit the target – although it was very small and a long way away. I was slowly getting better and let the last one fly. It was punctuated by a crisp, sharp sound as the arrow penetrated its target. I was delighted and turned around to share my excitement. Everyone, except Samantha, who was jumping up and down giggling, stood in stunned silence. Slowly, quietly '*Sugoi... Sugoi ne*' started to break the silence and then eventually the *sensei* came over and with a deep bow, congratulated me. I wasn't quite sure what the fuss was. A young *nidan* came up to me. I had chatted her up during a break, despite me being in the country for only five more days. She was very cute and I couldn't resist.

'Follow me,' she said, as she led me to the target area. 'It is very important you pull out your first hit.'

'Why was it a big deal about hitting the target?'

She stopped, looked deeply into my eyes and explained, 'I have been doing Kyodo for four years, hold the rank of second degree black belt and train three times a week, but I have never hit the target. I am very impressed and so is everyone else. We have never seen a beginner do this, let alone a *gaijin.*'

As I pulled out the arrow, she took my picture. I was also allowed to keep the target and the *sensei* signed it for me – apparently he was a senior member of the Japanese Kyodo Association.

Afterwards we had a few drinks in the clubhouse and an elderly member came over to me. I think he may have been a senior member of the *dojo* who no longer taught. He congratulated me on my achievement and said that I would never forget the sound and the feeling of hitting the target... and to this day I still can remember it. I understood then that maybe *kyodo* and karate were not so different. The form of karate I had been practising these past two years was the extreme, but the karate I loved, the karate I remembered, embraced all the same values that these *kyodo* practitioners were sharing with me now. I had so little time left in Japan, but it all seemed to be coming together.

My final week arrived. I still had not heard anything about my *yondan* or instructor status. They knew I would be setting up the

JKS in Ireland, but I had decided not to share the trip to the USA with them. I thought it didn't quite fit in with the story of me having to return home for financial reasons. The money problem was an issue, but before that, the issue of taking a real holiday for the first time in over ten years was greater.

On the Monday of the last week, Yumoto Sensei told me to come to the *dojo* on Saturday afternoon for a farewell party. I had gone beyond worrying if the farewell party was a euphemism for them bashing the hell out of me, getting their last chance in. Things had changed, so I was pleased that we would have a chance to say goodbye. My farewell party with my friends was planned for the Sunday and although I had invited Sueki, Hirota and a number of the *hombu dojo* students, I had not mentioned it to my *sempai* ; I thought I was too insignificant for them to bother with.

Saturday came and I walked into the *hombu* to be greeted by all the *sensei*, including Taguchi Sensei. Tables had been set up with mountains of food, just like we did at the end of *kangeiko* every January. Students had glasses of beer in their hands ready to make a *kampai* - the Japanese, guttural version of 'cheers'. I was quickly handed a beer and Yumoto Sensei gave a speech. I had never seen him smile, use complimentary words and say my name in the same sentence. I was overcome with surprise, panic, shock and delight. Yumoto Sensei talked about how he remembered me when he had taught at Ishii Sensei's house in the UK over ten years ago and how I had sacrificed a lot to move to Japan. How I had entered the instructors' course and trained hard, eventually graduating... did he say graduate? He finished with wishing me luck in Ireland, followed by the most booming 'KAMPAI' I had every heard.

I wandered around my *sempai* and *sensei* thanking them for coming, for doing this for me. Parties like this, in the *hombu dojo*, with all food and drink provided, were reserved for only very special occasions. In fact I had only been to three before now, two after *Kangeiko* and one when we had the official opening of the *dojo*. This was a big deal. When I got to Shima Sempai, after

190

the overlong, customary, 'Thank you ever so much for your continued kindness' and the short, 'No problem' response, almost as an afterthought, he said, 'Oh, by the way, here you are...' He opened a large file and pulled out three certificates. The first was a certificate of membership starting the following year for JKS Ireland affiliation. They had already drawn up all the paperwork and affiliated me for free for my first year.

'Wow... Thank you, *sempai* that is very kind.'

The second was a certificate for *yondan*. I had passed. As you get higher up the grades, dan tests can be very expensive and I had been worried that if I did pass *yondan*, I wouldn't be able to afford it. However, they had graded me for free. The final certificate was a handwritten certificate by Taguchi Sensei. Taguchi Sensei was also famous for his *Shodo* – Japanese calligraphy. Flowing and dynamic with powerful strikes and slashes, people often said that his *karate-do* and *shodo* were exactly the same. Of course it was all in Kanji and I couldn't read a word. Shima Sempai read it out for me. It was my certificate of completion. After two and a half years, I had completed the infamous JKS instructors' course.

What did I feel? It wasn't relief. I wasn't ecstatic, or over the moon, or overcome with pride. Like so many accomplishments in my karate life, on an emotional level it was nothing major. Logically, I was happy. Few triumphs in karate are tangible, but this one was. But I had come to realize that karate is only full of beginnings, never ends. This was simply a new beginning. I now faced the challenge of moving to Dublin and trying to teach karate full time. No one had succeeded in Ireland before me. I was broke and had no idea how I was going to set myself up, so the success of finishing the course was somewhat overshadowed by the massive task I faced. On the other hand, when I received the certificate I remember thinking that I could now die happy. I was twenty-nine years old and the rest of my life was stretching out in front of me, but I truly felt that what I had achieved could be enough. Of course, I wasn't going to allow myself that luxury, but even now,

191

ten years after graduating I can still find that feeling inside me. And I think I will never lose it.

At one point Takahashi Sempai found out about the party I would be having with my friends. He was angry and upset, almost emotional.

'Why didn't you invite me?' I didn't have an answer for him and I realized that out of all the people who I had trained with, Takahashi Sempai had put most effort into my progress. I felt as close to him as I did to Sueki. Of course, it was a different type of closeness, but all the painful memories I had of him had disappeared into some Stockholm-syndrome-type delusion. He had to leave early, so asked if I would be at training on Monday. I explained I had packing to do and this would be the last time I would be at the *dojo*. We shook hands and as we did, he leant across, almost hugging me, and whispered, 'Don't ever forget what you have learnt here and you will be fine.' I wanted to cry. Strong words spoken softly.

One by one my *sempai* and *sensei* came to say goodbye. Each had something kind and caring to say to me. Yumoto Sensei said he expected me to make them proud in Ireland and I promised I wouldn't let them down. They made sure I knew their mobile numbers – ironic, as the last two years of my life had been punctuated by their calls, commanding me to do something or berating me for not doing something else. Once I confirmed that I had their numbers, I was told that if there was anything I need, *anything*, I had to call them. They were all sorry to see me leave and, although I couldn't believe it, the feeling was mutual. As the students left, I was given small presents. Tamata-san, the student who I had forgotten to call *san* all that time ago came over to say goodbye. As he did, he handed me a black belt he had had made. On one side was written Scott Sensei, which was unusual, as normally *sensei* is never written on the belt. I think he was making a point to those who had stopped me teaching. On the other side were the characters for JKS. And on the reverse was written 'A gift from Tamata' followed by the date. All the embroidery was done in pure silver thread. It weighed a ton. It was a very expensive belt and what could I do but say, 'Thank you very much.' Why can't you hug Japanese people?

Naito-san, another *sempai* of the *dojo* came over and took my certificates. He owned a gallery and said that he would send them safely to my parents' home – he didn't want them to be damaged in transit. When I eventually returned to the UK, the certificates were there, all framed in beautiful antique, lacquered Japanese oak, with real gold edging. They now take pride of place in my *dojo* in Dublin.

The party finished and I went home. The day was no different from any other day I had spent in Japan. A mixture of emotions churned around inside me. I was happy and sad about leaving. I was excited and nervous about my future. I felt enormous pride and at the same time indifference about finishing the course. Would it ever be simple?

Over sixty people came to the farewell party for my friends, including the two guys from the local convenience store and the video shop. I was one of the few *gaijin* who lived in the area and had got to know them over the years. I had mentioned that I was leaving and they had asked if they could come to the party. I had spoken to both of them almost daily for four years and they had seen me in the worst times, but had always been kind, with an innate cultural understanding of what I was going through. They came, had a great time and both shook my hand vigorously, wishing me luck when it came time to leave. At some point I stood up and said a few words of thank you. Looking around I realized how much of a network I had developed during my time in Tokyo. At times I had felt so alone, isolated and detached, but now was different. The instructors' course had only been one battle but I had been victorious on so many fronts. For many of my English students this was the first time they had heard me use Japanese, but I was fluent and said everything I wanted to say without worry, in a natural – some said perfect – accent. I was moving into the unknown. I faced political problems with Ishii Sensei, financial problems (which could prohibit me from doing anything at all) and problems from the karate world at large. Were they going to accept a western karate *sensei*, especially one so young and only a *yondan*? One thing I had learnt from the course and my time in Japan was the knowledge that nothing was impossible. All I had to do was try my best and be happy with the results.

Three days later I left Japan. Handing over the *gaijin* card that I had kept in my wallet for the last five years, I severed my last physical connection with Japan and boarded the plane to LA.

The End

Postscript

I am an identical twin. My younger brother has always been bigger than me. When we were born, I came out first but was a full pound lighter than my brother. I had exhausted myself trying to get out first and had to go straight into an incubator. The midwife looked at me and said, 'Mrs Langley, you have a fighter on your hands here!' I guess she was right.

Terms used in the book

Izakaya

A Japanese bar/restaurant. The Japanese very rarely go to bars just to drink. Instead they prefer to disguise their binge-drinking by going to an izakaya and claim that their two small dishes of food between ten people constitutes eating out.

Christmas Cake

Japanese people often refer to women over twenty-five as leftover Christmas cake. Once past Christmas Day (the twenty-fifth) no one wants to eat them anymore!

Shou ga nai

It means something like 'it can't be helped' and is used for the most insignificant event to major disasters. I came to see it as people really not caring what happened or how things turned out in their lives, or the lives of others.

Gambatte ne

Try hard! Try your best! It is a phrase that is often used and the nuance, in this case, was that Shima Sempai was worried about me.

Hoitsugan

Infamous in the karate world, students from all over were allowed to stay in dormitories at the Hoitsugan dojo as long as they train daily there and at the hombu dojo – like a cross between a youth hostel and prisoner-of-war camp.

Genki
This is used all the time to mean full of life, lively, well – anything positive in a physical way.

Sugoi
Next to genki, sugoi is the most-used word in the Japanese language. (I can't believe I have got this far in the book without using them both.) Sugoi means terrific, great, brilliant – anything positive in a non-physical sense.

Kangeiko
Cold training. Starting on the last Monday of January many members of the dojo would meet at 7 am, jog around the streets and then return to train until 8 am. Continuing for a week, on the Sunday we would jog to the local Shinto shrine, pray for good luck and then return to the dojo for a party. It's a way of building dojo spirit.

JKA
Originally all shotokan karate was controlled by a group called the Japan Karate Association. The founder, Nakayama Sensei, died in 1987 and Taguchi Sensei was made Chief Instructor. However, following disagreements with the administration director in 1989 the JKA split and two fractions were formed. Taguchi Sensei headed one fraction, and a ten-year legal battle followed for the right to use the name. Taguchi Sensei conceded in 1999 and we had to change our name to JKS.

Made in the USA
Lexington, KY
31 January 2016